DREAM CHASING

Dr S.B. Misra was born in 1939 in a remote village in Uttar Pradesh, from where he inched his way, armed with brilliant academic credentials, to faraway Canada where he discovered 565-million-years-old fossils that plugged questions in Darwin's theory of evolution and made him an overnight star in academia. Four years on though, on the verge of fame and fortune, he quit that life and returned to his village where, soon accompanied by his newly wedded wife Nirmala, he set up a school that changed thousands of lives. He has since worked as a geologist and taught students in Lucknow and Nanital. He now lives as a retired professor in Lucknow with his wife. Both still run the school.

Neelesh Misra, Dr S.B. Misra's elder son, is an award-winning journalist who has written four bestselling books, is a Bollywood lyricist with major hits to his credit, heads India's first writer-led band, writes film scripts, is a photographer, has a hugely popular national radio show on which he tells a story every day to an estimated 20 million listeners from an imaginary city called 'Yaad Sheher' (Memory City). He is also trying to set up a rural call centre and a rural newspaper based out of the same village to which his parents dedicated their lives.

OTHER LOTUS TITLES

Ajit Bhattacharjea	*Sheikh Mohammad Abdullah: Tragic Hero of Kashmir*
Amarinder Singh	*The Last Sunset: The Rise and Fall of the Lahore Durbar*
Anil Dharker	*Icons: Men & Women Who Shaped Today's India*
Aitzaz Ahsan	*The Indus Saga: The Making of Pakistan*
Alam Srinivas & TR Vivek	*IPL: The Inside Story*
Amir Mir	*The True Face of Jehadis: Inside Pakistan's Terror Networks*
Ashok Mitra	*The Starkness of It*
Dr Humanyun Khan & G. Parthasarthy	*Diplomatic Divide*
Gyanendra Pandey & Yunus Samad	*Faultlines of Nationhood*
Lt Gen. JFR Jacob	*An Odyssey in War and Peace*
M.J. Akbar	*Have Pen, Will Travel: Observations of a Globetrotter*
M.J. Akbar	*Kashmir: Behind the Vale*
M.J. Akbar	*The Shade of Swords*
M.J. Akbar	*Byline*
M.J. Akbar	*Blood Brothers: A Family Saga*
Maj. Gen. Ian Cardozo	*Param Vir: Our Heroes in Battle*
Maj. Gen. Ian Cardozo	*The Sinking of INS Khukri: What Happened in 1971*
Madhu Trehan	*Tehelka as Metaphor*
Mushirul Hasan	*India Partitioned. 2 Vols*
Mushirul Hasan	*John Company to the Republic*
Mushirul Hasan	*Knowledge, Power and Politics*
Nayantara Sahgal (ed.)	*Before Freedom: Nehru's Letters to His Sister*
Nilima Lambah	*A Life Across Three Continents*
Sharmishta Gooptu and Boria Majumdar (eds)	*Revisiting 1857: Myth, Memory, History*
Shashi Joshi	*The Last Durbar*
Shashi Tharoor & Shaharyar M. Khan	*Shadows across the Playing Field*
Shrabani Basu	*Spy Princess: The Life of Noor Inayat Khan*
Shyam Bhatia	*Goodbye Shahzadi: A Political Biography*
Thomas Weber	*Going Native: Gandhi's Relationship with Western Women*

FORTHCOMING TITLES

Jaiwant Paul	*The Greased Cartridge: Heroes and Villians of 1857*
The Indian Express	*The Prize Stories: Best in the Indian News Business*

ONE MAN'S REMARKABLE, TRUE LIFE STORY

DREAM CHASING

DREAM. HOPE. BETRAYAL. GRIT. SACRIFICE. TRIUMPH.

by
S.B. Misra

as told to
Neelesh Misra

Foreword by Sam Pitroda, who created India's telecom revolution

LOTUS COLLECTION
ROLI BOOKS

Lotus Collection

First impression, February 2011
Second impression, April 2011
The Lotus Collection
An imprint of
Roli Books Pvt Ltd
M-75, Greater Kailash II Market
New Delhi 110 048
Phone: ++91 (011) 4068 2000
Fax: ++91 (011) 2921 7185
E-mail: info@rolibooks.com; Website: www.rolibooks.com

Also at
Bangalore, Chennai, Jaipur & Mumbai

ISBN: 978-81-7436-819-5

Typeset in Arno Pro by Roli Books Pvt Ltd
and printed at Rajkamal Electric Press, Haryana

contents

dedicated

To my wife, Nirmala

foreword

The generation of Indians that left India for North America in the 1960s in quest of a better education and therefore, by implication, a better life all seemed to have been made of the same mixture of grit and naiveté. I know because I was one of them, having left a corner of India that would not even qualify as obscure.

While reading *Dream Chasing: One Man's Remarkable, True Life Story*, the memories of Dr S.B. Misra I could relate to so many references from his early childhood in the India of the 1940s and 1950s that I felt that in some sense the story could well have been mine. 'I had never owned a watch, never combed my hair under an electric bulb. And I could not speak or understand English properly,' Dr Misra writes early in the book. This could have been true of so many others. In fact, it was true of so many others. Some of those managed to rise well above that.

The book has been consciously and somewhat self-effacingly described by the author as the story of an ordinary Indian. That sets it up for a compelling conclusion as Dr Misra, a geologist of repute, takes the reader through the drama of having discovered over 500-million-year-old fossils around Mistaken Point, Newfoundland, in Canada in 1967. What adds the twist to the story is how the credit for his seminal work on Ediacaran fossils was denied to him, not once but twice over a period of nearly four decades.

Dr Misra's story is inspirational for those Indian professionals who toil away from the limelight only because they believe in something bigger than themselves. In a country obsessed with just Hindi cinema and cricket it is important to tell more such stories, if only to tell India's 550 million below the age of 25 that there is so much more to explore and discover.

I have for long advocated the need for biographies, autobiographies and memoirs as a device to share with the future generations the thrill and romance of nation building. I hope Dr Misra's book becomes an important part of that.

Sam Pitroda
Chicago

acknowledgements

The idea of writing this book was conceived by my son Neelesh Misra during a seminar in New Delhi. He heard stories of many individuals and organizations narrating their stories of social contribution. Without telling me, he went to his office and prepared a book proposal that he sent to Roli Books. I have always been reluctant to glorify myself either as a geologist or as a social worker. But Neelesh had given me a 'fait accompli' – I had to tell my story, I had no choice. This book is culmination of that idea.

This book is also a response to the curiosity of colleagues over the years – including eminent scientists both in India and overseas – over how the 565-million-year-old fossils at Mistaken Point in Newfoundland were discovered and what happened to my career in the years that went by. This book is for those who might be curious about the discovery and the discoverer, about conditions in the Avalon Peninsula, Newfoundland of those days and hardships and vagaries of climate then.

The biggest thank you is for Zara Murao who helped put the story together. I express my heartfelt thanks to her for her consistent effort at editing, data collection and re-writing of the manuscript of the book.

My wife Nirmala Misra has not only helped give shape to the fanciful dreams of my childhood, but also contributed in great measure in completing the book. Many of the faces I had forgotten, or incidents that had faded in my memory, were reminded by Nirmala who also helped interact with them to complete the story. My close friend V.V.N. Simharao has not only been a selfless supporter of my projects and ambitions for forty years; he contributed his impressions and wrote his life sketch that has been incorporated in the book. He continues to be on the same wave length as we are and understands our cause and commitment to rural education.

During the writing of this book, Prof. Hank Williams in the Memorial University of Newfoundland very kindly added to information about the university administration of those days. I have fond memories of his painstaking editing of my historic thesis that had reported my discovery.

Dr Penny Blackwood, Director, Alumni Affairs and Development, Memorial University was kind enough to help in locating some of my old friends and showed interest in writing a story on me in the LUMINUS, the university's alumni magazine. Diane Guzzwell, Assistant to Department Head, Dept of Earth Sciences took the trouble to provide information about the department. I appreciate their help and cooperation. Donald J. Fitzpatrick, who had assisted me in the field during 1967 still remembers me and Inn Koh of South Korea. I remember them all with appreciation and warm feelings.

I express my gratitude and profound appreciation to Dr Hunting W. Brown, Director of Sustainability, Wright State University who helped me, always happily, in making lots of literature available to me.

And last but most certainly not the least, I would like to thank my childhood friend Ravi Shanker, who recently retired as the Director General of the Geological Survey of India. He shared many stories of childhood days including the ones I was either unaware of, or had forgotten.

prologue

The huge iron gates opened and we drove in – a bit nervous, a bit fidgety, feeling quite small in the sprawling, palatial Raj Bhavan – the colonial-era official residence of the Uttar Pradesh governor. It was 11 a.m. on a warm September day in Lucknow, the city where my wife Nirmala and I had spent much of my life. We were probably as nervous as our driver Surendra Singh, who had never been to any place even remotely as grand. My wife sat on my left in a sari she had spent a long time choosing that morning. We tried to hide our nervousness and kept on looking outside the window – at the beautiful gardens, fountains and tall trees on both sides of the road leading to the main building. It has always been a spectre of splendour – the huge campus was once the regional headquarters of the British army, with its grazing pastures, stables, chandeliered halls, picturesque statues, fountains, retained its charm. A fountain depicting the state government seal, statues representing the holy rivers of Ganga, Jamuna and Saraswati, a pair of leaping fish and a marble umbrella add to the beauty of the compound.

I had often seen this imposing, intimidating building when I came to my bank nearby. I used to see the huge Iron Gate, the immaculately dressed guards standing there, and the endless looking expanse of gardens visible through the gate. I had passed many times by the road running along the boundary of the Raj Bhavan. But today, I felt like the poor Sudama might have felt when going to the palace of Lord Krishna.

We were here because of a phone call I received the previous morning.

'Hello, am I speaking to Dr S.B. Misra?' the male voice had said.

'Yes, speaking,' I answered, assuming it was a journalist. Journalists had been kind enough to write a lot about me for much of the previous week.

'I am calling from the governor's office,' he said. 'Governor Sahib would like to meet you.'

I was as excited as a child. 'When should I come?' I asked. Is tomorrow convenient to me, he asked. It was. 'I am fixing the time at 11 a.m., please come 15 minutes earlier at the main gate,' he said.

'Will they allow me to come in as I will have no letter of permission with me,' I asked. I wanted to make sure that I had no problem.

'I will arrange that,' he said and the conversation ended.

I was overwhelmed and in the fit of excitement I forgot to ask if I could bring my wife along. I tried to guess the duration our meeting would be, the subjects we would discuss, the papers and photographs I should carry with me, even the posture I should sit in.

I excitedly told my wife that we would go to the governor's house the next day.

As usual, she asked, 'What shall I do there?'

The question was quite expected, and my answer was ready. You remain with me and give your opinion if it is something that concerns you. She finally agreed.

'What should I wear?' she said.

As if I knew – I had to change clothes all the time just before leaving for some place, because my children would disapprove and say they didn't match, or were not the right colour. Nevertheless, I tried to give five-paisa worth of fashion opinion. Didn't quite work – she wore the sari that one of our two sons had gifted her the year before.

We had reached the big Iron Gate on time. Several reporters had also come there to cover the meeting, an exercise that a reticent retired professor like me was just not used to, although my elder son and daughter-in-law are both journalists. They checked from the governor's office and allowed my car in, but said my wife could not accompany me. I was irritated, and it showed. Finally they agreed to let her in. The reporters wanted to go in as well, but they were refused entry.

We drove in, and our car stopped in front of the main building, an opulent 200-old structure called Kothi Hayat Baksh (the life-giving mansion).

We were greeted by officers and staff of the governor. 'This way sir,' one of them said. Walking a few steps, to my left was a big hall where I was asked to occupy a seat on the sofa. They ushered my wife in a different direction: 'Madam, please sit here.' She was left behind, sitting in another room rather uncomfortably – and visibly disappointed.

'If this is so, then I might as well go back without meeting the honourable governor,' I told the governor's aide-de-camp (ADC). After a few minutes, my wife entered the hall and joined me. The governor had broken protocol and came out himself to meet us in a most cordial manner. We spoke for about an hour. He talked about the story of my life, narrated in some details by the newspapers. Then he felicitated us with a bouquet – and the waiting journalists appeared at this time, as if out of nowhere.

As we stood blinded by the camera flashes, I thought of the one person in the room who was almost denied this moment – my wife – the one person without whom this long, long journey would never have been completed.

It began with my long walk to school.

a sickle and a dream

On 22 May 1939, months before the Second World War broke out, Adolph Hitler, the German Reich Chancellor, and Benito Mussolini, the dictatorial ruler of Italy, sat across a table to sign a pact between Nazi Germany and Fascist Italy.

That, of course, has nothing to do with this story.

That very day, thousands of kilometres away from the room where those world leaders signed what was called the 'Pact of Steel', an old midwife raised an iron sickle to cut the umbilical cord that attached me to my mother. This is how most children were delivered in my country way back then. In my village of Deora, in the heart of northern India, it was a service she provided at every childbirth.

Perhaps it was the sickle, perhaps just my destiny, but I got critically ill soon after I was born. It was not that I was born a healthy baby. As the cord was severed, the women in the village began wailing in mourning, believing I was stillborn.

It was one of the many cycles of destiny through which my life would pass. Decades later, when I became the father of twin boys, my elder son Neelesh would also be born apparently lifeless, only to be revived by my mother-in-law with a solid thump on the back.

One of the women in my village, Kunti Bua, put her prestige on the line and announced that she would bring me to life. She put a red-hot bead to my forehead and, is it any wonder, I began crying. I would bear that mark for the rest of my life, but I did survive.

My village was set up by my great-grandfather, Adhari. He moved there with his new wife some time in the mid-nineteenth century, to a home he built with his own hands. The two-room mud hut faced east for luck, and was adjacent to two ponds, so there was plenty of water. He had two sons and two daughters. When the daughters married, he invited his sons-in-law to settle nearby, and as the settlement grew, Deora was born. Social differences were not bitter in those days, as they are today, but as was the practice the village came to be divided on social lines. There were four distinct quarters; for the Brahmins, where my forefathers lived, Yadavas, lower castes and the Muslims, respectively.

My great-grandfather had two sons, Jagdeo Misra and Chakradhar Misra (my grandfather, popularly known as Chakkar Maharaj). They were good cooks and went to the house of the local landlord each day to cook for him. My grandmother, Chakkar Maharaj's second wife, was blind. She had four sons, of whom only one, my father Balbhadra, survived. Two died of childhood illnesses; a third was buried alive when the mud roof of their home collapsed. Following that, my grandfather no longer addressed my father by name, referring to him simply as Ladke (boy).

My grandfather farmed land, raised cattle, and made sweets for a living. As a teenager, my father's duty was to go to nearby villages to collect milk for the sweets. This could take hours: he had developed such a sweet tooth by then that he would fill his pockets with sweets before he left the house, munching along the way. The moment they were finished, he would set the milk utensils down by the roadside, run back to the house, fill his pockets again, and run back to resume the journey. Of course, no one in those days was aware of diseases like diabetes and I am certain all the running around burnt all the calories anyhow, as there was no TV and computer games to while away our days and keep us rooted to the sedentary couch as children are wont these days. As a child, my father was a very good student. His teachers all said he was very promising, even though he had little time in the day to study. Every morning he loaded sweets on a horse and delivered them to the nearby towns of Mahona and Itaunja. Then he would rush back to attend the primary school at the nearby village of Amaniganj, leaving his horse to graze on the fields outside.

As his workload increased, his father decided the boy could not be spared for the classes any longer, so he was taken out of school. It would be unfair to say my grandfather was hard on him. Education was not a priority in those days, though it had been a priority for my father.

Others in his class would do just about anything to get out of studying. One of his classmates, Banshi, would jump up every so often in class and tempt the teacher: 'Maulvi Saab [Teacher Sir], shall I run to the pond and fetch you some fish?' Banshi sometimes got away with it and the teacher had a decent dinner. My father, by contrast, dreamt of completing junior high school, a lofty ambition for a village boy in early twentieth century India. I think I inherited that yearning to study from him. Had he, however, ever hoped to rejoin school, his marriage soon ended all that. He never entered a school again, except in the final years of his life when he lived in one all on his own. As for the other boys in the village, none of them made it to Class 5, the highest class at the school.

I remember nothing of my mother: her name, face, voice. She was hard-working and soft-spoken. It was said she washed utensils so well they glittered like jewels. As with all other women in the village, she had to get up early in the morning to grind grain to prepare flour, sweep the house, scrub the utensils and cook. She worked so hard and yet was not treated well by the family. She suffered from ceaseless fever and became bedridden after a prolonged illness when I was still an infant. Her father took her to her village of Misirpur, and there she died.

She did witness my name-giving ceremony. My family summoned a pundit a few days after my birth to suggest a name. He suggested Shiva Balak, the welfare-giving child. In India, all names have a meaning and significance. In some parts of the country the name of a person includes the name of the father and even grandfather, to hint at lineage. Elsewhere, it indicates the place to which one belongs. The belief is: '*Yatha namey tatha guney* (as the name, so the virtues)'. The name-giving ritual is performed with grand ceremony. I'm glad my mother was there.

After my mother's death, I stayed with my maternal grandparents in Misirpur. My maternal grandmother (or nani) was very fond of me and wanted me to stay with her for good. By the time I was a few years old she had collected a large number of silver coins to be used in my *yagyopaveet*, the thread ceremony performed to initiate an upper-caste teen into the Hindu religion.

My father and grandfather had sent repeated messengers asking Nana and Nani to send me back to my village, Deora, but my maternal grandparents wouldn't. They doted on me and perhaps also did not wish to send their daughter's only child back to the home where she had been so callously treated.

In Deora, my father and paternal grandfather were getting impatient, and eventually decided on an audacious plan: to kidnap me! It was not a decision they easily took. After all, the British colonialists ruled India with a stern hand and all crime was punished swiftly and severely. Even so, my father did not want to lose his only child.

I have no memories of being abducted, but the elders of my village tell me that a lot of planning went into the strategy. My father and grandfather got together many strong young men. It was a carefully calculated risk and they were aware that there was no real manpower on my grandmother's side, and knew too that she could not go to the police citing kidnap by a parent. All that was required was to get me out of her house without a fuss.

Early one morning, a group of seven or eight people, led by my father, packed some *puri* (fried unleavened bread) and fried vegetables and set out on their perilous mission to Misirpur. The distance alone was a significant hurdle: they had to travel 16 kilometres and return the same day lest I be recaptured.

At the village of Ataria, they bought the sweets they knew I loved. A kilometre from my nani's house, my father and one of the musclemen advanced while the rest hung back. A crowd would immediately attract attention.

It was past midday; time for the second part of the plan. The rest of the group now walked up to the village and hid just outside. My father knocked on the door of Nani's house, just as he would on a regular visit. He hugged me and gave me the sweets. I was thrilled to see him and we chattered as he led me out to the courtyard in front. Suddenly, he reached out, grabbed me in his arms ... and ran!

The kidnapping was successful. They rushed back to Deora before I knew what was happening. I think the year was 1945. I was six.

Some time later, my father decided to remarry on the advice of the village elders. I was not treated badly by my stepmother but there seemed always to be a wall between us. In the years to come, my stepmother would have several sons, but many of them died at an early age. Two of her sons and three daughters survived, and I remained to them a brother and fatherly figure.

I had now settled in at Deora, made new friends and forgotten all about Misirpur. It was all play and no work for us kids; children began school late in those times and I was still too young to be saddled with odd jobs or chores.

Around us, the struggle for Independence was climaxing and everyone was looking forward to the joy and promise of a free nation. The people of my village did not know much about the fight for freedom or the remarkable men that led our struggle. All they were aware was that the *goras* (foreigners) would soon be gone. They knew, too, of Mahatma Gandhi. In fact, an elder in my village, Hardeo Bajpai, used to call me 'Gandhi Baba' because I was so skinny!

Some time in the summer of 1946, I had my *paati* puja, a ceremony that marked my initiation into learning. The stars and astrological charts were consulted and an auspicious day chosen. It was quite a ceremony when the child was given a *kalam* (a pen made of a bamboo twig), *budika* (a chalk solution in a small bottle) and *takhti* (a wooden slate with a handle). The pandit performed his puja and held my hand to guide me in writing the name of Lord Rama on the wooden board. Who cared for the letters? All we wanted were the sweets at the end.

Soon after the ceremony, I was assigned my first teacher: my illiterate grandfather. He might have been unable to read and write, but over the years he had come to appreciate the importance of education. Way before I began going to school, I had learnt from my grandfather how to count up to a hundred, recite *pahada* (multiplication tables), some stories and poems. My family was thrilled when I bedazzled others by showing off my knowledge.

I remember how a grand old lady from the village, Danai Dai, gave me a one-paisa copper coin when I stood before her, not nervous at all, and was able to count up to a hundred in a loud, clear voice. I had still not started school.

Good lord, when they think you are bright, everyone wants to test you. 'If there are four camels standing with their faces facing east, west, north, and south, how will you make them eat from a single basket?', Baijnath Bajpai, a village elder, once asked me. On another occasion, he asked: *'Teetar ke do aage teetar, teetar ke do peechhe teetar, teetar–teetar–teetar, kitne teetar?* (Two partridges in front of a partridge, two behind a partridge, partridge – partridge – partridge, how many partridges?)'. If, however, all this made me overconfident, that pride was soon to be crushed when I ran into my first big speedbreaker: Urdu.

People of all religions studied Urdu then. It was not seen as only the language of Muslims, as politicians have made it since. Urdu was the language of the courts and revenue records and my grandfather wanted me to learn it. Urdu was a big deal. Off I therefore went, with two other Brahmin boys, to the house of Chhatrapal Singh, a private tutor in the nearby village of Karuwa. Singh knew Urdu well. It was a commonplace image of those times that seems so out of place in today's India so divided by religion and language: three Brahmin boys learning Urdu from another Hindu.

Singh began teaching me the Urdu alphabet: *aliph, be, pe, te, se, jeem, che, he, khe, daal, zaal*... I was clearly not cut out for this, forever forgetting the subtle differences in the letters and misplacing all the dots. Two weeks after I began my classes at Chhatrapal's house, I still had no clue about what I was doing. The scoldings and punishments only made it worse, and soon I had made up my mind. I gave up the language for good.

However, I had a plan. 'I want to go to school,' I told my grandfather. So, in late 1946, at age seven, my grandfather decided it was time for me to go to school. My first schoolteacher was called Zalim Singh, whose name literally meant 'Cruel Lion'. He was a Dalit, the lowest caste in the Hindu social hierarchy, and taught at a makeshift school 2 kilometre away in Kunaura village.

Zalim Singh was of medium height, dark-skinned, and always wore a dhoti, kurta, and sandal-like shoes without laces. He topped the outfit with a white cap, a walking stick, and looked perennially solemn. His school was a single-teacher establishment where children could study up to Class 3, and he often passed our fields on his way there.

One day, as he was walking by, neatly attired and stern-faced, my grandfather called out to him and asked him if he would round up all boys in the village, take them to his school and admit them as students. Zalim Singh considered, and found the idea not without merit. He took us all along and entered our names in the admissions register.

Most of us, of course, did not know our dates of birth. No one kept such records in those times; many still don't in rural India. Zalim Singh therefore invented a birthday for each student who did not know his own. I was really proud that I knew mine.

Now that I was in school, with my name and date of birth noted down in a big, official register, I was certain great things would follow. It didn't matter to me that my school had no building.

Classes were conducted under a thatch roof in the house of a Dalit family. There was a box in which the attendance registers were kept, some jute mats for the students to sit on, and a charpai for the teacher. I do not know if the house owner was paid any rent by the government, but he was never seen to grumble; nor did Zalim Singh either, and although he had to walk 5 kilometre to the school every day, he was never late. For the record, he was cruel only in name. Zalim was tender-hearted, never stern. He certainly never beat us; something very common until recently in Indian schools.

Only four students actually attended his school from my village: three other Brahmin boys and I. We walked the 2 kilometre there and back every day, along a narrow path through a thick forest. The route was quite frightening. The elevated narrow path through the waterlogged area during rainy season was difficult to negotiate. If we failed to pay attention to the *pagdandi* along which we walked the scorpions that escaped from the water would welcome us, and if we did not look around, there were wild animals to scare us. Wolves and jackals would emerge from the dense bushes and cross the path, their narrow eyes freezing us in our tracks.

It's a good thing they never attacked, for it would have been virtually impossible to outrun them, especially as we were barefoot. We had shoes, but they were preserved for special occasions. If there was a wedding or a feast, we would wear our black shoes and a white Gandhi cap. I actually thought school warranted both, but my father disagreed.

the long road ahead of independence

Then one morning when we awoke we were a free nation. Even in my dusty nowhere village, miles from New Delhi and Parliament house where Pandit Jawaharlal Nehru had given his stirring 'tryst with destiny' speech, Independence was a festival, like a village fair. Everyone was suddenly and proudly wearing patriotism on their chests. It was a wonderful feeling.

Scruffy farmers in well-washed wrinkled clothes marched through their villages holding aloft the national flag, our very own national flag, and singing '*Jhanda ooncha rahe hamara, vijayee vishwa tiranga pyara* (May this flag always be held high; this tricolour that has won over the world)'. School-going children began greeting one another with a loud 'Jai Hind! (Long Live India)' when they met, and repeated it once more when they said goodbye.

On 15 August 1947 the entire population of the twin villages, Deora and Karuwa, gathered near the village *pradhan*'s house, sweets were distributed, and the flag hoisted in my village for the first time.

There was a profound respect for khadi then. The homespun fabric, together with the Gandhi cap, were symbols of who we were and the remarkable way in which we had won back our country. Our politicians were our heroes. I still remember the names of at least three Congress party members from our area. There was an authority in their voices; a ring of integrity and selflessness. One of them, Janki Prasad, went on to become a member of the state level Congress committee. Villagers loved to hear tales of the prominent Congress leaders he had met.

Back then, there was an unbelievable passion among people to rebuild their nation, even with their bare hands, as it were. In many cases, that's exactly what they did, offering *shramdaan* (donation of labour or work for no pay). The mud road joining Deora village to nearby Karuwa was built by such volunteer workers in two days flat. Then the people of my village got together to dig feeder canals to the fields without being paid any wages. This spirit of collective action continued for many years.

Back at my school, however, things were not looking good. Zalim Singh had been transferred from Kunaura, and several months on there was still no replacement. My impatience was growing. My father therefore took me to Atrauli, my stepmother's parental home, to enable me to pursue my primary education.

It wasn't an easy journey. We walked about 15 kilometres to Basahari Ghat, then crossed the river Gomti on a small rowboat (meant to seat 15 but routinely loaded with up to twice that many, in addition to everything from bicycles to goats, and even baskets of chickens and vegetables). Then we walked another 15 kilometres!

You could say I had moved up in life. Compared to my village, Atrauli was a big deal. This was a large village, with several people in government service. Back in Deora, or even Kunaura, the larger village nearby, a government chowkidar, wearing a red *saafa* (turban) and khaki uniform and carrying a javelin, was a big thing. In Atrauli, there were several shops; back home, there had been just one shop for our cluster of villages, where the fat, partially sighted, Jodhe Sah would barter salt, sugar, and condiments for grain.

Atrauli was known to have a very good primary schoolteacher – the tall, soft-spoken Bhagwati Prasad Shukla, who taught me very affectionately in Class 2. The village was famous also for a man called Ram Vilas Tewari, who used to trot about on a white horse followed by several musclemen on foot. This man was the big boss of the area, having earned the frightened respect of the people, and he resolved disputes amongst the farmers, his decision being final.

I began a new life in Atrauli, in a new school. I did not have to carry roasted gram in my school bag any longer because I could go home for lunch during the break. I had more time to study now. Soon, I had memorized tables up to 20, besides learning other tables called *pauwa* (multiples of a quarter), *adha* (of half), and *pauna* (of three-quarters). These were most helpful in day-to-day life then, but are redundant in today's age of computers and calculators.

I was happy in Atrauli with my new friends, a bigger school, and still larger village. My step-nani (maternal grandmother) was a stocky widow full of affection for children. She had four daughters. Her mud house was immaculately clean and well kept. I had all the time to study there. I was addressed by elderly people as the son of Chandrakali (my stepmother) and that is how I learnt her name. In north India, women are not addressed by their names in their *sasural* (in-laws house).

My life in Atrauli was exciting, but proved to be short-lived. In the summer of 1948, I developed *badi-mata* (smallpox) and my father took me back to Deora.

Now, I was back among my friends, who had, in the meantime, shifted to the primary school at Amaniganj, the large village where my father once went to school on horseback.

Amaniganj was 4 kilometre from Deora, not an easy walk for a ten-year old. On the long trudges to school, we would amuse ourselves with riddles or poems. Sometimes, we caricatured students and dramatic events from our school, such as the latest beating of one of our classmates. On other occasions, we would pretend to be warriors and throw *dhelas* (lumps of mud), scrambling over each other to see whose had gone farthest. Sometimes, if it was a close call, shrill arguments would break out, to be settled by a series of precise measurements using sticks or twigs.

Once in a while, we had *dhela yuddhas* (mud-lump wars) between students from different villages, but these were friendly battles, always waged at a safe distance so no one was really hurt. If a piece of mud hit a boy from the opposite camp, everyone would rush over to see if there was likely to be a bruise. After some prodding and apologizing, we would solemnly declare it the end of the day's battle.

The following year, at the age of eleven, I had my *yagyopaveet*, the sacred-thread ceremony. There was a public feast and new clothes were given to the entire family. The sacred thread brought certain privileges: people of other castes would now say '*Pranaam* (Greetings)' to me with reverence, to which I would respond '*Khush raho* (May you be happy)'. It also brought obligations, such as a daily bath before the first meal and remaining *maun* (silent) while eating.

If the sacred *yagyopaveet* thread was intended to take me to a higher plane and give me access to the gods, it was just in time. I needed all the help I could get: danger lurked in every corner of every home... Snakes and scorpions sat smugly in the walls of our mud houses, comfortable in holes made by rats. There was no medicine available for snakebites and if, God forbid, someone was bitten, he had to depend on God's mercy to save him. Some local people claimed they could cure snake bites by chanting mantras while beating metallic vessels and drums. It was however by the grace of the gods, and the snakes, that only one or two people died of snakebite in my area when I was growing up. The snakes, especially the deadly King Cobra, were allowed to escape. They were not killed by villagers, who celebrated a festival in their honour every year on Naagpanchami, the fifth day of the month of *Shravan* (August).

Sitaram Tewari, of nearby Karuwa village, claimed to know a mantra that could defeat the poison of the scorpion. He would whisper a chant and rub the affected area. I had been stung by scorpions several times and went with my grandfather to him on each occasion. His chanting seemed to offer me some relief, though the pain of the sting persisted for two or three days.

I always wondered what he said; which kind god he was invoking to rid me of the pain. It was only much later that I discovered Tewari had been muttering abuses all those years, not mantras. In hindsight, I think it was probably the massages that made people feel better.

The other insect that stung quite often was the *tataiya*, a yellow (if female) or purple (if male) wasp usually found in mango orchards. The sting caused a swelling and a burning sensation that remained for up to two days. We were of course not the only ones at risk.

Pythons often lurked in the thick bushes outside the village, snatching a calf or goat ever so often. While we would run a mile if we heard a python was around, the cowherds had learned well how to deal with them, even though most of them were no older than twelve.

The cowherds were usually the many children in the village who could not go to school. They had to help support their families, so they worked in the fields or took cattle to graze in the forests. To while away the time, the cowherds played games like *siar-satkana* (hanging like monkeys from a tree) and *surbagghi* (a game similar to Chinese checkers) using sketches on the ground and pebbles. The older cowherds supplemented their income by making ropes of bark and grass, collecting firewood, gathering grass for brooms and animal feed, and plucking wild berries. They asked the younger ones to mind their animals.

The cowherds did not fear wild animals. One day, a python began swallowing a deer calf. The cowherds beat the reptile till it died. They then took the dead python to Karuwa, the calf still alive, wedged half in and half out. They cut open the python and took out the calf. The cute little baby deer was nursed by one Badri Tiwari of Karuwa and the deer remained with him for many years, I was told recently by elderly villagers during my visit to my village.

Twice a year, the entire male population of the village would meet for a community meal. Everyone ate in a single area, though in caste-wise clusters. On one *amavasya* (the day before a moonless night) in May, they would assemble in a large open area in an orchard north of Deora to roast lumps of dough on a fire made from dried cow dung. On the other *amavasya* they carried *sattu* (flour made of roasted barley and gram) and ate together in a single area. The huge gathering of all castes and religions cooking in assembly and eating together maintained the sense of separate communities living in harmony. The children played as the food simmered.

I had chores, like every other son in a farmer's family. I was in charge of carrying jaggery or roasted gram and water to the labourers working in our fields. The labourers were mostly Harijans (People of God, a term Gandhi coined for Dalits). The caste system and its rules were so deeply ingrained in our behaviour that the labourers would not touch the water vessel I carried. I poured the water into their folded palms, as they glugged from their wrists. They seemed to accept this naturally then, but today would refuse to drink water rather than accept it in this way.

My other jobs included sitting on the bullock-driven leveller to add weight, picking out grass and weeds from the fields, etching out the corners and sides of fields, breaking large clay boulders, and carrying implements from our home to the fields and back. It was hard work, but the breaks were fun: we usually ran off to the nearest orchard to ferret away fallen mangoes.

I lived the life that urban India would only glimpse in films for a long time to come, in *Mother India* or one of the Dilip Kumar films. It was a life of crushing poverty, just like hundreds of millions of other Indians in faraway villages, but also a life of contentment. I was not aware of the material comforts in towns, and quite frankly I didn't really care, and never would.

For young me, perhaps the most tedious job in the village was the threshing and winnowing of wheat. Dried wheat plants were cut from the fields with sickles, tied into large bundles, and dumped at the *khalihan* (threshing ground). There, the bundles were unfastened and the contents spread on the ground and a pair of bulls walked on the stalks in circular motion, hour after hour, day after day, in the most oppressive heat. It took three or four days to separate the grain from the chaff in each lot.

After the harvest, it was time to make the payments for various services rendered through the year. All payments were made in kind. Bundles of wheat were therefore given to the barber, the washerman, the gardener, blacksmith, and carpenter. They were landless and took one bundle from each farmer, thus gathering enough to last them through the year. The two pundits, Gyandas and Ramdas, at the temple near our mango orchard would receive pure grain instead of bundles of wheat.

Also, just as in all the Bollywood films, the feudal landlord or *zamindar* was the big boss. All land rights were vested in him; the farmer was just the *seerdar* or tiller. The landlord of my village was Jagdeo Singh of Dhaunrahra village. After each harvest, his musclemen would walk through the village collecting land revenue, paid in large quantities of pure grain, according to the extent of landholdings.

The lower castes were worse off, often forced to slave on the *zamindar's* land without wages. The musclemen would leave a small bundle of grass on the thatched roof of a lower caste family, a sign that the man of the house was needed for work on the landlord's property. The next day, the man would dutifully scurry off to carry out the appointed task. This practice continued until the abolition of the *zamindari* system in 1954.

While in the fields, my Baba (grandfather) would narrate tales from Hindu mythology to me. There were many times when I walked long distances with him. That's when he told me his best stories. Those were the moments when I learnt some of life's best lessons: simple things like the importance of conquering fear and being courageous.

Once, he told me, he was riding his bullock cart around midnight when the bullocks suddenly stopped in an orchard west of the village of Dhilwansi. The orchard was believed to be haunted. He tried to coerce the bullocks, beat them with a stick, twisted their tails, but the stubborn bulls just wouldn't budge.

Baba climbed off the cart and tried to push it, even recited the Gayatri Mantra (the most auspicious hymn of the Hindus) repeatedly, but in vain. He was now getting suspicious that evil spirits were around. He was about to leave the bulls and make a run for it when he noticed that one of the bullocks was shifting uneasily on one leg. A rope had got entangled the bullock's hoof and, once it had been freed, the cart started moving again. Perhaps the evil spirits were watching and having a good laugh, Baba liked to joke.

There were only occasional opportunities for entertainment in our village. Different castes and communities had specific programmes. Dhobis had the *dhobiha* (washermen's) dance, depicting stories of their life; upper caste Hindus organized Ram Lila performances, plays based on the legend of Lord Rama, during the Dussehra festival every October. The other sources of entertainment were *nautanki* or theatre and shows staged by snake-charmers, *baazigar*s (magicians), acrobats, and performing animals like monkeys and bears.

These joyous moments are etched in my memory, but so is one less joyous when I developed a large boil on my left thigh at the age of twelve. It was surgically removed in the village without anaesthesia by Dargahi baba, a layman barber armed with just a cutthroat razor. As three men held me down, screaming and flailing, he lopped the infection off in one clean sweep. At the age of seventy, I still bear the scar on my left thigh.

After the operation, he covered the wound with a paste of ground neem tree leaves and salt. The bandage was changed every day. When no *pus* appeared at the spot, he added some honey to the dressing and left out the salt. That was a relief.

By and large, people were healthy and diseases were rare in those days. The mightiest and most feared was tuberculosis, nicknamed *raj rog* or king of all diseases. Malaria was tackled through natural perspiration by covering the patient with a large number of quilts. A concoction with some local herbs, such as the leaves of the medicinal herb *tulsi,* black pepper, and ginger, was also administered.

This was, however, akin to a common cold compared to the deadly outbreak of cholera in the late 1940s. It began in the quarters of the leather workers and spread to every house in the village. I still remember Shiva Kumar, a gentle boy who had come from Mahona town to visit his maternal uncle, and had gone into the jungle with the cowherds. He returned with unstoppable vomiting and loose motions, and died in less than three hours. Dozens of others died before the village head called his doctor friend, Vaidya Daya Ram, from Lucknow to inoculate the villagers and control the disease.

From Atrauli, my stepmother's maternal village where I had stayed earlier, there was even worse news: the plague had arrived, I heard elders whispering among themselves, one quiet, mauve evening. The first sign of the Black Death was the mounds of dead rats, that were supposed to be burnt. The only precaution suggested was to wear knee-high socks so the *pissu* or 'tiny organisms' could not reach the skin. When the disease reached Atrauli, the village was evacuated and everyone moved to an orchard. Weeks later, a huge fire was lit and every house, shop, and cowshed burnt down. Animals and a few belongings were allowed to be salvaged. The following year the villagers returned, to build new homes.

nearly wed

It was 1951 and young India was preparing for her first election the year I completed Class 5. Our nation and I had both passed a major milestone: India had a constitution in 1950; I had my Class 5 report card the following year.

However, the real battle for both of us loomed on the horizon. For the men behind India's new constitution, the real test would be India's first democratic election. Would I make my career or be failed by the new India, like Ramdeo Azad of Kumbharawan, who along with his wife were jailed during the freedom struggle? Their son was born in jail. His house was razed to ground by the British rulers yet he did not get a ticket for the first election in new India. Would I succeed in getting a ticket, in my case admission to class VI? For me, the victory of getting the highest marks in my school was marred. I was now as educated as my father but my scholastic career was facing the same fate as his.

The odds were stacked against me and it seemed as if I would have to give up my education, the thing I cherished most. At the age of eleven I had been able to easily walk the 4 kilometre to Amaniganj and back every day. Now, however, it was time for junior high school, and there was no middle school, as it was called in those days, at Amaniganj. The nearest ones were at Kumbharawan and Itaunja, 12 kilometres away.

My father and his friend Puttu, whose son had also passed Class 5 that year, had lengthy discussions about what was to be done. One evening, they sat at the *chabutara* or gathering place in the village square, to weigh the options; curious villagers gathered around, each offering solemn advice.

***

The *chabutara* was an earthen platform near the common well in Deora. In one corner was a large neem tree. Below the tree there was a pile of round stones from a nearby riverbed, representing Lord Shiva.

The neem tree has since been uprooted and the stones shifted to the centre of the platform. The pucca well, though poorly maintained, is still in use. In those days, only caste Hindus could sit on the *chabutara* and Dalits or Scheduled Caste villagers would take their places on the ground.

This was no ordinary seating place. The *chabutara* was witness to the resolution of many village disputes. This included many thefts, though the methods of investigation would not exactly have met with the approval of the Central Bureau of Investigation.

If something was stolen and a woman was suspected to be the thief, all the women would be given grains of rice to chew. It was believed that the thief's jaws would not move and she would instantly be identified. If a man was suspected, all men would be asked to lift *Shankar ji ki batia* (the rock representing Lord Shiva) by turns. The one whose hand trembled was usually assumed to be the thief.

As a child, I often wondered how it was that all 'thieves' were toothless grannies or women with bad teeth, and weak ailing men with less than the required strength in their biceps. The best way to stay out of trouble in Deora, I told myself, was to brush your teeth regularly (using the neem twig, as was the practice in those days) and have plenty of proteins to build up those muscles!

***

So, at the same *chabutara* where justice was doled out and disputes settled, began the most important negotiation of my life. I of course was not involved, but everyone else seemed to be getting into the spirit of the thing. Finally, over the hubbub of voices as everyone offered suggestions and tutted at the lack of options, one man made his voice heard. 'The path to Kumbharawan passes through the forest; the road to the Itaunja school is cleaner and the education is also better,' he said.

So it was decided: my neighbour and friend Raghubar Dayal and I would go to the Itaunja school. A few days later, Chheda Yadava of Pandit Purwa village came to our house for advice from my father, a good friend, about his son Ashrafi Lal (his name literally meant 'son of a gold coin' ... no one knew why) who had also passed Class 5 and wanted to study further. Ashrafi Lal was two or three years older than us and well built, so when his father asked if the teen could walk with us to Itaunja we were only too happy to oblige.

When the new school year began, the three musketeers, Ashrafi Lal, Raghubar Dayal, and I, went marching off to the junior high school in Itaunja town for admission to Class 6.

In a room facing the main gate, a tall, heavy-set man with a twirling moustache sat solemnly in a chair. This was the headmaster, the legendary Munshi Sharda Baksh Singh, one of the most respected teachers in the entire district. We froze in our tracks, petrified. As we stood face to face with Singh, we remembered all the fearsome tales we had heard about this man, who some said was feared by the children ten times more than the plague.

Down a corridor to the right, past the row of classrooms facing the gate, a peon indicated where Munshi Bhim Singh was taking admissions to Class 6. Munshi Bhim Singh, in his white dhoti and brown kurta, was a friendly face. We had no problem or fear in striking up a conversation with him. Behind the building was a large open ground with mango trees, a pucca well, and a pond to one side. At the far end was a boarding house. It seemed like heaven. Within minutes, we were the newest additions to the school. Regular classes would begin the following day.

The longest walk of my life had begun. Every morning, I trudged three hours to my new school. Every afternoon, I walked the 12 kilometre back home. For the first three months, classes began at seven in the morning, so we began walking at 4 a.m. We had of course to guess the time because no one in the village had a clock.

On some full moon nights, we would wake up hours early, thinking it was time to start for school. Halfway there, we would realize our error, but by then there was no point in going back to the village. We would therefore walk to school in the dark and sleep in the playground till the peon came to open up the school. Even when we got the time right, it was too early to eat, so we took little packets of roasted gram and jaggery to munch along the way, saving some of it for the midday return journey.

Long walks angered and frustrated me. I often grumbled: 'Why can't there be a school near my home?' I had a school bag, but it was nothing like the school bags my children would use. It was an ordinary cloth bag of the kind used in middle-class homes to carry vegetables and other groceries from the market. The bag had become heavier in Class 6, and when the weight of it caused our shoulders to ache, we would carry the bags on our heads.

The morning walk was not as uncomfortable as the return journey, which started just after noon. We were hungry and thirsty by then, and the heat was scorching. Along the path home, thankfully, was a Jain shrine where a bucket and rope were always kept on an open well for thirsty travellers to take a cool drink. We invariably stopped there for a break.

The drink would not however last us till Deora and, near the big orchard in the village 3 kilometre before ours, we would have to stop again. Here there was a well, but no bucket and rope. We therefore plucked large leaves off the Dhak tree to from a bowl. Then we would weave long strands of grass together to make a rope, tie the leaf bowl to one end, and lower it into the well. It was tedious work, because the water would drain out through the joints as it was being pulled up and only a tiny amount would remain. It took many attempts to get a decent drink.

It was a little better between October and April, when we had all-day school. We would start at 7 a.m. and we could have breakfast – leftover rotis (unleavened bread) or rice with milk, sometimes jaggery and roasted grain *laddus* (sweets) – before we started out, and carry something for the midday meal. We couldn't carry cooked food, there still not being sufficient time to fire the wood stoves and cook a meal. We did, however, take the sweets made of roast grain and jaggery and sometimes I can still taste them if I close my eyes. Alas I cannot eat them any longer as I have become diabetic.

Of course, once we got home, there was the homework. That was never easy. During the morning school months, we were tired and sleepy by the time we got home. The rest of the year, the long walk meant it was near sundown and there would be no light in which to read.

The walk home became even more difficult after village elder Lachhman Bajpai discovered that the big orchard near the well in the next village was haunted. Bajpai was passing by at midnight, he told the village folk the next morning, when the branches of a tree crashed to the ground a few feet away. Then, he saw two men walking out of the orchard in spotless white clothes. After that, none of us would walk past the orchard alone, not even at midday. The detour was longer, but at least it wasn't haunted.

In the monsoon, the long walk was hell. The roads were all muddy and slippery. Raincoats were unheard of and umbrellas were not common. At many places, the road would disappear under water through the three months of the rainy season. In some places, the water was knee-deep or deeper and one could not differentiate the road from the fields. Sometimes, we were drenched after the first five minutes or so and would trudge miserable and cold the rest of the way.

Once, Lachhman Bajpai, the same village elder who saw the ghosts, gave me three rupees to buy 3 kg sugar from Itaunja for his grocery shop. On my way back, I toppled into one of the water-filled ditches, sugar and all. As I watched the syrup drip out of the bag for the next 4 kilometre, I wondered what he would do to me and how I would ever repay such a large sum. When, however, I gave Bajpai the packet, he didn't say a word. He didn't even complain about how much of the sugar had dissolved in the water. He was a good man, Bajpai. I was glad the ghosts had not harmed him.

Another good man was Bhola. Short and stocky, he sat near the gate of our Itaunja school, selling spicy *chaat (*boiled gram garnished with spices and condiments) by the roadside. Bhola was from Dharampur, a nearby village, and was famous for his cleanliness, good nature, and punctuality. He would serve his *chaat* on a large leaf and we sometimes bought some for two paise per head before heading home.

Twenty-one years later, I returned to Itaunja for a visit with my wife Nirmala, Bhola was still there with his *chaat*. His face lit up when I told him my name, and he asked about the other boys. Guess he had a good memory too.

* * *

Munshi Sharda Baksh Singh was perhaps the best teacher I ever had. I sometimes think it was because of him that I so wanted to be a teacher myself.

I remember so many little things about him. He was fond of smoking the hookah but would never smoke in front of the students or teachers. He would go to a room at the back of the school, where a peon would prepare the hookah for him in the interval. His school was everything to him. He returned to his village 3 kilometre away in the morning and evening only for his meals. The rest of his time was devoted to his students, coaching the weaker ones after school hours free of cost.

Over fifty years later, I met his son Batukeshwar Dutt Singh, who had also studied at the Itaunja school and was seven years my senior. Batukeshwar retired as a government officer in a development block near Lucknow, the state capital. He had built a large house, like that of an old-time zamindar (landlord), back in his village. However, in the courtyard at the back, he had preserved two mud rooms exactly as they had stood decades ago; the rooms where his father Munshiji used to rest and do his reading. Inside, Batukeshwar showed me dusty photographs of the stern-looking man. Our teacher; principled, kind-hearted, and a man who had touched thousands of lives.

Another favourite teacher from Class 6 was Munshi Bhim Singh, the man who had admitted me to the Itaunja school. He was famous for punctuality and discipline, and yet I often reached his class late. Munshi Bhim Singh understood the difficulties of my long walk and never scolded me for it.

As for me, I had gradually settled into the new routine, and every now and again, the exhaustion and monotony were broken by that great, big, all-Indian ceremony that entire village still looked forward to for months: a feast. Sometimes it was part of a religious ceremony, sometimes to mark a death anniversary. Once, in 1952, a rich sweetmeat-maker from Babaganj, a town near my village, arranged a feast on the occasion of a public meeting addressed by Govind Ballabh Pant, a national leader who was then chief minister of our state of Uttar Pradesh. Streams of people came to squat in lines to eat *puri* (the fried unleavened bread was a special treat), *subzi* (vegetables), and sweets, and listen to the speeches.

I went with others from my village. As I ate and listened, I couldn't understand most of what Pantji said, but he was a marvel to watch. He had a bulky physique, but it was his posture that made me curious. I finally asked an elderly person sitting near me why Pantji shook his head all the time. He whispered that once, when the British police were showering blows on Pundit Nehru with their truncheons, Pantji threw himself on top of the future prime minister of India and took all the blows on his own head. Since then, his neck shook all the time.

It was tales like this that earned our political leaders such great respect in those days, as did their austerity and honesty. Rafi Ahmad Kidwai of my district, though a minister in the central government, was in debt when he died. Pundit Satya Premi, also of Barabanki, had only a cot and a few wooden chairs in his drawing room even though he was a legislator.

Politicians were honest and observed austerity. Living was cheap, but all that was about to change. Wheat, land – and dowry – would soon become multi-crore industries. With that, the gap between the haves and the have-nots would widen to a chasm. Wheat is forty times dearer now than it was when Pantji gave that speech but agricultural land is about a thousand times more expensive.

The farmer, for whom the founders of our nation fought so hard and planned so zealously to protect, has been sidelined, his fertile fields parcelled off to the highest bidder for untold millions.

Some things have of course changed for the better: somewhat. Child marriages, which were common and were seen as a status symbol in those days, are rare today. Ah, child marriage. They say it is an atrocity against young girls. What about the young boy! I can still vividly remember that Sunday in the winter of 1952. I was in Class 6 and a group of four or five people came to my village in a solemn procession. They had seen me walk to school every day and thought I looked healthy and promising. They wanted me to marry Putti Lal Dwivedi's daughter, then about ten years old.

I remember three charpais were arranged near the *chabutara*. On one of them sat the guests, on the other two were people from my village, including my father and grand old Shiva Govind Bajpai, who always had the last word in my village. Shiva Govind, the father of Lachhman Bajpai, would live to be ninety-five, a miracle in our times. He did not know the year of his birth, but used to say he was born during *badkawa jhura* (the big drought).

I remember being called to join the men at the *chabutara*. I had heard ladies in the house saying '*Dekhua aaye hain*' (people have come to see the boy for marriage). I was really nervous. I came forward with a gloomy face and looked with pleading eyes at grand old Bajpai, like a sacrificial lamb looks at the butcher. He, however, convinced my reluctant father to accept the proposal. Dowry was negotiated at Rs 600 The girl's side even gave 10 per cent of the amount, along with the *nazar* (token money in respect), to the village elders.

In one evening, my life had turned upside down. It was the greatest obstacle my scholastic career had so far faced. How could I possibly go to college in the big city if I was supporting a wife and, oh Lord, perhaps even children? I sat alone and cried all evening. I did not even eat that day, but who cared for the lamb crying alone in his room?

After some weeks, the father of the girl realized he would not be able to fulfil the conditions of dowry and conveyed his inability to our family. He was scared the advance money given by him would have to be forfeited, but my father happily returned the entire sum; he had after all accepted the proposal unwillingly.

Looking back, I wonder what became of the girl. Things could not have gone well for her after news spread that her father did not have enough money to pay dowry. Perhaps she ended up with a much older man or a widower; perhaps even a cripple. As for me, I hate to say it but I had never been happier. The god of schools had won this round and I imagined the god of marriage was probably sulking in a corner up in Heaven.

As I walked to school the next day, I said a quiet prayer of thanks to the former, and apologized contritely to the latter.

* * *

I had dodged the untimely marriage, but the long road to school still shackled my feet, and I was getting virtually no time to study. I completed the oral portion of my homework during the return journey. I would open the notebook or the text and read while walking. Fellow students would tell me to keep reading loudly or talk on one subject or another. I would walk ahead of them, talking as we walked, my friends listening like disciples. Once I was done, the others repeated what I had said and I would correct them wherever necessary. This method of learning proved very effective for me too: I began developing a deeper understanding of my subjects. I was, however, getting no time to complete the written homework, and the long hours of walking were telling on my health. In desperation, I told my father: 'I will lag behind in class if I continue walking like this every day.'

He appeared to understand and went to Mahona, 8 kilometres away, to talk to Sundari, the widowed sister of our neighbour. She agreed to let me and my friend Raghubar Dayal, who was actually also a distant relative, live with her.

That reduced the walk somewhat. We would contribute 20 kg of rations and some lentils to her every month. The arrangement worked wonderfully. Sundari cared for us like a real mother would have. She was gentle, affectionate, and caring, and would tell us charming stories and mythological tales to relax our minds and teach us good values. Sometimes she would tell us funny stories to make us laugh and it was as if we were a real family. I was in school, happy. Life was good.

Then, in April 1953, I got chickenpox for the second time and I could not take the final examination for Class 7. I was shattered. As soon as I could walk, I set off for the headmaster's office, walking all the way in the blazing sun, covered all over in blisters. My friends told me I looked like an alien. My class teacher, Pandit Brahmadin, was moved when he saw my condition. I could see that he really wanted to help. He said that if the headmaster, Munshi Sharda Baksh Singh, agreed, he would conduct a separate examination for me, away from the other students.

I was quaking as the headmaster inspected me, but he agreed and my examination was arranged separately in a hostel room. I had saved myself from forfeiting an academic year. They said it was the most unusual thing to happen in a school headed by Sharda Baksh Singh. Then came my toughest examination ever: the final year of junior high school, the toughest of all the classes.

There used to be a board examination at Lucknow for Class 8. There were night classes for which students had to stay in the school overnight, going home only in the evenings and mornings for meals. The frequent walking back and forth was again becoming a terrible nuisance. I therefore decided to find a place at Itaunja, near the school. I moved to a boarding house where students could live for a nominal charge and were allowed to cook their own meals. We had, however, to bring our own *charpais* to sleep on and our own utensils to cook in, our own wood for fuel and lamps to light the room at night. There were four students in each 80 sq. ft room. However, a teacher was available to guide students as and when necessary.

Pandit Brahmadin, the warden of the boarding house, could not stand straight due to a physical condition but maintained strict discipline. His little daughter lived with him at the hostel; his wife had died and he was bringing her up on his own. Decades later, he met me in Lucknow, where I had built my house and was bringing up my two sons. He had not forgotten me. 'Shiva Balak,' he said, 'the jackfruit tree you planted in the boarding house is still there and giving fruit!'

Shyam Narain Misra, the English teacher living in the same boarding house, was a harsh man of primitive thinking. '*Ghar ki marammat saalana, ladke ki marammat rozana* ('A house needs repairs annually; boys need it daily),' he would say.

At fourteen, all this was a completely new experience for me. The boarding house was full of life and we cooked meals in groups of two or three boys, segregated, sadly, in those days by caste but without any ill will. Common meals were less time-consuming and more economical, so we shared our ingredients and firewood.

My distant relative Ram Raghubir came from a sandy area of the Gomti river belt where wheat, millets, maize, and lentils were the principal crops. He brought flour and pulses. My village was in an area of loamy soil where rice was the principal crop, so I brought rice and vegetables. We cooked meals on mud *chulhas* (earthen stoves) using firewood.

I used to envy Ram Raghubir, who had once travelled in a train all the way to Ataria station. He used to describe the joy of his train journey. I had never seen a train in my life! Not even a bus or a railway station. The boarding house let me satisfy at least one of those ambitions. Itaunja was a small town, but it had a railway station only half a kilometre south of our school. One evening, soon after I moved to the hostel, I went to the railway station with Ram Raghubir. I was overwhelmed by the sight of the signalmen controlling train movements.

I was however unable to board a train, and it would be some time before I was able to taste the luxury of train travel. It was April 1954, to be precise, when all the students of Class 8, about 80 in all, travelled to Lucknow for the final exam. It was my first visit to a big city; a journey of discovery. I sat mesmerized in my window seat, watching the houses whiz past, the trees along the railway track, and the trucks plying on Sitapur Road, running parallel to the railway line. It was about an hour's journey with stop-overs at Bakshi-ka-Talab, Mohibullapur, and Daliganj. We got off at City Station and headed for the Arya Samaj Mandir in Rakabganj. We stayed in Lucknow for ten days. We contributed rations and some money to the common mess. For every exam, we would walk about 2 kilometre in a line to Aminabad Inter-College, our exam centre.

This was an entirely new world. I saw an electric bulb for the first time; streetlights that made the city glitter as if it were day. I saw running water in taps. As I looked up at the lamps at Itaunja railway station, I thought of Deora, groping in the dark. My world was changing.

Little did I realize what was to come. Two months later, in June 1954, a classmate of mine came running up to me as I relaxed in our ancestral mango orchard (I call it an orchard, but it actually consisted of only twenty trees) in Deora and said the result of the Class 8 Board exam had been declared in the newspapers.

I rushed to school next morning and found that I had topped. After a year of great physical hardship and poor health, it was the greatest gift I could have received. I was now as educated as all my teachers. I had made it to my first goalpost. I still had not however learnt to dream big. In an educational survey in my class, we were all asked: 'How far will you study? 'I wrote "High School", Class 10 being the most to which I could aspire. Perhaps I was afraid to hope for any more.

Armed with my high school degree, I told myself, I would become a revenue officer, a police officer; perhaps even a malaria inspector.

one hundred and twelve rupees

I was wrong. There would be no revenue officer's job; not even a malaria inspector's. That summer, the summer of 1954, appeared to be the dead end of my educational career. There was a huge speedbreaker ahead: 40 kilometres ahead, to be precise. That was the distance to the nearest high school. It was all the way in Lucknow, the alien city where I knew no one and there was no one to take me in or guide me. My father could not help me out either. He had lived briefly in Lucknow, but it hadn't been a happy experience. He had chased a dream too, travelling to Lucknow long years ago and finding a job as an assistant to a *vaidya* (ayurvedic practitioner) in Chowk, one of the cultural hubs of the city. He used to help the *vaidya* grind, sieve, and pack the powdered medicines. Then my father suffered an electric shock. Shaken, he returned home to Deora, the jolt having weakened his right thumb, and his resolve. He went back to milking his cows and buffaloes, and even that wasn't easy, thanks to his thumb. He was not a fan of Lucknow. He could not help me.

What made me even more miserable was that my classmates from the primary and junior high school had already set out on the paths they had chosen. Girija Shanker got married and moved to Kanpur to live with his father-in-law. He would complete high school and go on to be a food inspector. Raghubar Dayal went to the religious shrine of Naimisharanya, learnt Sanskrit, and followed in the footsteps of his father Puttu, eventually becoming a respected pundit. I was left alone to find my way, and was getting desperate.

One day, I finally told my father: 'Daddu (that is how I used to address him), I desperately want to study.' His brow furrowed and I could see he did not have a solution for me this time. My father had however never discouraged me before, and he didn't this time. He just sighed and said: 'Let us see, there will be some way out.'

That way out appeared in the form of a man with a squarish face and a short, stout body. This was Chhota of Khanpur village, a distant relative. Chhota had some idea of the city as he had lived for some time in Lucknow, running a student mess in one of the hostels of Lucknow University. He had given it up when the students stopped paying him.

'Uncle, you must do something,' I said in our local dialect. He responded, '*Lohe ka hath marab* (I will apply an iron hand to the problem).' He suggested that I stay with his nephew Partap, who had a small-time job in Lucknow. That was it: I did not ask him anything further; I just thanked him profusely and began packing.

I washed my clothes using the white-coloured *Rehu* (alkaline sodic soil); soap had not made it to the villages yet. I was so happy, but deep down, I was worried too. How would I meet my expenses in the big city? I really missed my grandfather, who could have managed funds for me but he had died when I was in Class 8. He was so caring and I had been wretched when he was bedridden for over six months. He would have been so thrilled, and so helpful, had he been alive.

Then my father worked a miracle. He somehow arranged for enough money for me to go to the city and pay my initial expenses. To this day, I don't know how he did it. I suspect he borrowed the money from Bharat Bajpai, the village moneylender who later became a saffron-clad sanyasi. My father also arranged for rations to last me quite a while:

about 10 kg of flour, 5 kg of rice, and 2 kg of pulses. The final piece of the jigsaw had fallen into place. Thanks to his help, I was finally able to take the reins again and resume my life. I began thinking of the city that I had seen when I was taking the junior high school board examination. My dreams once again came alive.

I carefully packed my marksheet and school transfer certificate. My stepmother carefully packed the rations. Then, all of a sudden, it was time to leave home. Leave my village to live in the city I had been so bedazzled by on my first visit. It's strange, but even at fifteen, I knew this was a moment that would change my life forever. When I returned, I wouldn't be the same person I was now. Perhaps I would return cynical, perhaps I would be a star. I naturally hoped it would be the latter. Either way, I knew there were new doors opening ahead of me, others closing as I walked through them.

I remember it was 1 July 1954 when I bade farewell to my envious friends, bowed my head to the pile of stones representing Shankarji at the *chabutara*, touched the feet of the village elders in the traditional gesture of seeking blessing, and left my village. My father, Chhota, and I walked from the village to Itaunja on the same endless path I had trudged every day to school. As I looked around, I could hear the echoes of our chatter, the three musketeers; see us shoving each other as we argued over some forgotten dispute. I could hear my own voice, repeating over and over the lessons we had done in school. You made it, I thought to myself. It wouldn't be easy going, and the big city might never be home, but you're on your way, Shiva Balak. I shifted the bag of rations from my left shoulder to my right. When the weight of it made my shoulders ache, I shifted it to my head. The rest of the time, my father carried it for me.

As we walked, my father gave me advice on living in the city. Don't trust too easily, he said, don't talk too much to strangers. Never lend money to anyone ... His voice trailed off as he ran out of tips, and a calm but charged silence descended on me. There was so much uncertainty, yet such excitement. So much gratitude too that I should have found a way to reach out from my dark village to the electric lights I never thought would be within my reach.

***

From Itaunja, the three of us took the evening train to Lucknow, and all of a sudden I was back in the city, this time to stay. To revel in the trains, electricity, running water. We got down at Daliganj station, then the northern limit of the city. Very few people lived here, most in the guava orchards west of Sitapur Road. The rest, now a bustling, chaotic part of the state's capital, was farmland. The market was small and a bridge made entirely of iron (called, well, Iron Bridge) across the river Gomti connected Daliganj to the rest of the city. I walked down the street brimming with hope and excitement. Chhota guided us through lanes and by-lanes to Partap's single-room house. Partap and his wife agreed to let me live with them, but he seemed to have more space in his heart than in his room.

Their room, about 5 m. long and 3 m. wide, was everything rolled into one: kitchen, bedroom, and drawing room. There was no toilet internal. I was given a corner to spread my matting and put my belongings. My father handed over the rations to Partap, left some money with me for my expenses, and returned to the village the following day with Chhota.

I do not remember how I decided to join college; perhaps it was Chhota who gave me the tip. I secured entrance the very next day to Government Jubilee Inter-College, with the highest marks of all the applicants. Getting admission proved to be easier than getting there: a 3 kilometre, hour-long walk.

The college was, however, like a dream. It had huge buildings with Mughal-style architecture and was situated right near the railway station in the heart of Lucknow. The buildings, with high ceilings and verandas, were built around a large, well-maintained playground. It had facilities I could never have dreamt of: laboratories, a library, and sports facilities.

If college was heaven, Partap's place was proving to be something else altogether. It was not congenial for a student. What bothered me was neither the walk, not really long by my fairly high standards, nor the lack of a toilet in the room, nor sleeping on the ground, or even the absence of electricity, for all these were everyday realities back home. My problem was that they were fighting all the time, and the smoke from the village-type mud oven, which used firewood, was killing me in the tiny room. Partap's wife thought she was beautiful: fair enough, I suppose, but she often made the most unreasonable demands of Partap, demanding that he buy her this thing and that, without a care for his limited income. I had no idea how to deal with this; an adversity for which I had not prepared myself.

My father returned after some weeks with rations, ghee (clarified butter), and clothes. I told him of the difficulty, but I felt helpless and disappointed when he advised me to continue, as he had nothing better to offer. Something else however came to my rescue: my practice of playing teacher to my friends.

I used to visit my old friend Ram Raghubir, who was living in a shop in Raja Bazaar with his brother-in-law, who made and sold syrupy sweets. I used to help Ram with Hindi, English, and Mathematics. His brother-in-law had watched me play teacher, and knew of my difficulties at Partap's place. He suggested that I stay with them. This was godsend; I moved at the earliest opportunity.

One battle won, I had another small one to go. I was still obliged to ask my father for money every now and again, and I knew he was borrowing from the local moneylender each time. Determined to stop this, I began to tutor a Class 6 student in Yahiyaganj every day in the evening for the grand sum of six rupees a month. My father continued bringing rations and ghee but now I was financially independent!

Back home, my village, the rural heartland of Uttar Pradesh, was rapidly changing. The run of the feudal lords ended, at least officially, in 1952, with the abolition of *zamindari*, an end to feudalism that gave the farmers rights to their land, provided the owners personally presented themselves before the sub-divisional court. All the people of my village went to the court, far away in neighbouring Barabanki district, to stake their claims. My father went with them, but discovered that the land was in the name of my deceased grandfather. The lawyer suggested that my father pose as Chakkar Maharaj (my grandfather). He retorted: 'Land or no land, I will not do that.' The land remained, but the rate of revenue increased.

Land grabs began. The forest that we had walked through on our way to primary school at Kunaura was fast disappearing. People were also swapping land, staking claim to fertile plots of the Forest Department and giving up barren land elsewhere in exchange. All this happened, of course, with the connivance of revenue officials or *patwaris*, who now regarded themselves as only slightly less important than god.

Puttilal, the *patwari* of my village, popularly known as 'Lala', once went to Lucknow by train and did not even buy a ticket. When the ticket checker confronted him, he said sternly: 'I am a servant of the government.' The railway official retorted, 'So what?' and promptly fined him. It became a big joke in the village: 'Lala Puttilal takes bribes from everyone, but the ticket checker took one from him.'

In 1953, believing they were indispensable, all the *patwaris* across Uttar Pradesh resigned en masse, trying to push for better salaries. Chaudhari Charan Singh, the revenue minister then, stunned them by accepting all the resignations and promptly appointing new recruits. That was another fairly popular anecdote in our village, told heartily and invariably ending in raucous laughter.

As for me, I was beginning to like Lucknow, or at least what I knew of the city. My one regret was that I had no travel stories to share with my classmates. Most of them were from the cities and often spoke about the historical monuments they had seen on Sundays and holidays. I decided to go somewhere and therefore decided to go one Sunday to the Residency, a historic monument. I saw bullet marks on the brick walls and a lot of graves. This was where the freedom fighters of Lucknow besieged about 3,000 British army officers and soldiers for months in 1857, during our first war of independence. For the British rulers it was mutiny.

The two Imambaras (Bara and Chhota), with a huge Rumi Darwaza in between, were from an even older era, the rule of the nawabs, the Muslim rulers. The Bara Imambara and Bhulbhulaiya (labyrinth), it is said, were ordered to be built by Nawab Wajid Ali Shah to create work for his famine-stricken subjects. It took years to build because the nawab paid the poor to build it in the daytime, and the more prosperous feudals, who were ashamed of engaging in manual labour, to demolish it by night, thus creating work for all.

In August 1954, applications were invited by the principal for fee concessions for students. I submitted an application and was granted a waiver of half my fee. The next year, when I was in Class 10, my class teacher, Waqar Ahmad Zafar, helped me get a full waiver, now enabling me to really enjoy my six rupees! And I was about to earn a lot more.

Urdu was the language spoken in Zafar's Muslim home in Katra Abuturab Khan, so he asked me to teach Hindi to his sons, who were almost my age, for ten rupees a month. I almost felt like a banker with so much cash coming in every few weeks.

There were hardly any students from villages in our class. There was Saktu Ram of Raipur, Awadh Prasad of Jugrajpur, Shamim Ahmad of Barhaidih, Ram Prasad of Jindpur, Mahbubullah Khan of Itaunja, and perhaps a couple more in a class of forty-five.

Ironically, it was usually the students from the villages who always studied with greater concentration and were invariably well-versed with their lessons. Even so, one of my classmates, Halim, who I remember as a short and stout city boy, once said to someone in the most offhand manner, 'The boys from the villages are really *ganwar* (gauche).'

I never heard anyone argue with Halim about that statement, but I certainly found it in very poor taste and avoided his company thereafter. Even otherwise, I remained reluctant to talk to city boys for months together until I established meritorious credentials in class.

It's true that we led very different lives and wore different clothes. In those days, people in villages wore a *saluka* or single-layered body-fitting wrap and a *bandi* or double-layered cloth lined with cotton. There were cloth strings to fasten the two. I had a *bandi* when I was in Class 5 and remember it keeping me really warm in winter.

So you could easily distinguish the rural boys from the urban ones. We village boys wore shirts, pyjamas, and leather slippers. The city boys wore shirts, trousers, and polished shoes. The urban boys were better informed about current affairs and trends because, though television had not arrived, they had the radio and newspapers in their homes and the privilege of guidance from their educated parents. The village boys lived like Spartans, and you could tell it in their eyes that they had survived against harsh odds. How harsh, the city boys would never know. Just as they would never know of the many who never made it; never had the opportunities they had; I had.

All around us, in the village and the city, were people from hundreds of castes and sub-castes, and different religions. Religion was not the great divider it has become today.

In my village, all the Muslims would take out processions on the annual day of Muharram (mourning). It was an event for the entire village, although Hindus did not beat their chests and most did not even know why Muslims did so. Hindus would however put up various shops of edibles for the Muslim devout. For us children, it was just another mela.

At the time of course the pain of Partition had not yet sunk in when lakhs of families were torn apart across India. Hindus were friendly towards Muslims, and vice-versa. Muslim elders in my village were addressed by Hindu children as Chacha (uncle) or Baba (grandfather), and they had as much right to scold Hindu children if they were found being naughty, as the Hindu elders could reprimand Muslim children. Now, in many parts of India, there are riots over something as small as that.

I was enjoying my studies in Lucknow, and even having fun in class. The class of Maulvi Abdul Hakim was an occasion of particular humour and amusement. Maulvi Sahib, a robust man, would stride into class each day in his *churidar* and *sherwani*, recline as far as he could in his chair, and promptly fall sleep. When we saw this, we would begin talking, which would wake him up. Startled, he would shout '*Khamooooosh*! (Sileeeeeeeeeence!)' and go right back to sleep.

Then there was the tough cookie, Maulvi Nazawat Ali of Mahona, a lean and thin, active, agile, and smart teacher who had taught me art and craft in the junior high school at Itaunja. We had a history, Maulvi Nazawat and I. In school, I could take in all the maths and science you wanted, but art? That was a slightly hazy area. In college, this Achilles heel returned to haunt me.

Once, Maulvi Nazawat asked us to draw the mythical burning of Lanka in the battle between Lord Rama and the demon Ravana. Well, I tried, but it is safe to say that what I drew did not in the least resemble

Lanka or its burning. He was furious. He gave me three lashes of the cane on my palm and said: 'Shiv Balak! I don't care how good you are at *riazi* (mathematics), you will fail in art.'

I am happy to say I did not, but I guess it's something I passed on to my elder son Neelesh, who, as a student at St Joseph's College in Nainital, became the first in his class to ever fail in art; this was also the only time he failed a subject. You might think that was a bit excessive, but when asked to draw a portrait of Indian cricketer Surinder Sharma, he had drawn a likeness of Adolf Hitler! It was in his genes, I guess.

In college, I had an edge over the others in Hindi and Sanskrit given my schooling in Itaunja under Munshi Sharda Baksh Singh and my childhood lessons from my grandfather in traditions, culture, and Hindu mythology. My Hindi teacher in Class 10, R.B. Seth, was once so impressed by my Hindi explanation of a poem that he read out my paper to students in Class 12, two years my senior. That was my rebuttal of the mindset of classmates like Halim.

My best friend in college was Ravi Shanker, a peaceful, sober, and diligent boy who was brilliant in class but never boasted. We would study together at his house on Sundays and holidays till late in the evening. Ravi Shanker was from a well-educated family and lived in Chhachu Kuwan, not far from Raja Bazaar where I stayed. Ravi, with whom I am still in touch, was not interested in movies, was unassuming, and never tried to show off. His strong background in science and mine in Hindi and Sanskrit proved complementary during our combined studies.

His father, Ram Shanker Saxena, worked in the state secretariat. He was highly impressed by the socialist economic model and often cited examples from the USSR over dinner. It was in Ravi Shanker's house that I successfully fought a huge mental hurdle: eating in a non-Brahmin household. His family was from the intermediate Kayastha community and even ate meat!

As I was a strict vegetarian, Ravi Shanker's family would not eat meat if I was eating with them. Once, they were having lunch and I dropped by. Ravi Shanker's younger sister Ranjana had a piece of chicken in her plate and hid it in her hand. Her dog Jimmy, sitting at her feet, thought he was being offered the piece and gobbled it up. Ranjana was really sad, Ravi Shanker told me, when he narrated the incident to me much later.

Another amusing incident had occurred around that time, and this I would only learn about four decades later. One day, on his way home, Ravi Shanker was passing the sweet shop where I lived when he saw me helping lift a *kadhai* (large deep pan). The sensitive boy was distraught. He thought I was earning my living and paying for college by working at the sweet shop. Ravi Shanker went home and narrated the incident to his mother, and she felt so sorry for me that she cared for me ever after with the greatest kindness.

That is perhaps why she always gave me the love I liked to think my real mother would have lavished had she survived to bring me up. I still remember the chilly night in January 1956 when she gave me a blanket. I was studying with Ravi Shanker and wearing only a half-sleeved sweater. It was sufficient for me because I was used to the biting cold of the village, but his mother could not bear to see me in it. She brought me the blanket, draped it over my back, and insisted that I take it with me. I treasured it for years.

* * *

I had always wondered whether my ambitions would take me as far as becoming a malaria inspector; well, I soon got to stay with one when I shared a room with Tribhuvan Singh of Atasua village.

Tribhuvan lived in a small room, one corner of which served as the kitchen. There was a small cot in another corner and texts and notebooks in a third. Tribhuvan was doing a part-time Bachelor of Arts degree, and he was a malaria inspector.

His success, my friends were fond of solemnly recounting, was tinged with tragedy. His younger brother, Kunwar Bahadur Singh, my classmate at Itaunja in Class 6, had tamed a lot of pigeons in a hole in the mud wall of their village home. One day, the pigeons started fluttering about and cooing hysterically. Kunwar thought they were fighting and thrust his hand into the hole to quieten them. He was unaware that a highly poisonous snake had set the pigeons off. It bit Kunwar's hand and he died that very day.

By early 1956, the high school exams were just three months away and I was getting concerned. The long walk to college, cooking my meals, and giving tuitions to my student were taking up a lot of my time. I therefore approached Swami Yoganand of Yogeshwar Math and asked if I could stay at the *math* (Hindu monastery) till the end of my exams. He agreed! I didn't even have to pay, or cook; only the long trudge to the college in central Lucknow remained. My stay at the ashram in Naubasta in the south-western part of Lucknow was most comfortable.

Yogeshwar Math had a huge compound with several acres of mango and litchi orchards. There were cows, clean tube-well water, and a healthy atmosphere, just as in my village. Strict discipline was, however, maintained in the ashram. All of us had to get up early in the morning to clean our teeth with neem twigs, bathe, and assemble for prayers.

With healthy food and milk, fresh fruits and vegetables, my health improved considerably. Swami Yoganand was Bengali and used to play the *mridang* and sing melodious *kirtans* (hymns) in the mornings and evenings. In the morning, everyone had to do some yoga after prayers. It was a first for me, and sort of fun.

I was so busy that I didn't even have time for a haircut, so when I went home during the March festival holidays, my father and the rest of the villagers thought I had become a monk. The booming *kirtans* I sang, sitting on the *chabutara* on Tuesdays with the rest of the village, only reinforced their suspicions.

I guess I had got into the spirit of the devotional songs. I in fact still enjoy them, although I am neither fond of singing nor have the voice for it. My son writes lyrics for Bollywood films, and I am fairly certain he did not acquire that skill from me: probably from his mother, who is a very accomplished singer.

* * *

After the high school exams in April 1956, I wanted to go home for the summer vacation, but didn't have any money; not even enough to buy a railway ticket. I had stopped tutoring my student months before my exams, and I had spent all the money I had. I resolved not to beg or borrow, and so decided to walk home: 45 kilometre.

With a bag slung over my shoulder, I began walking from Lucknow on a hot summer day in the first week of May 1956. I had eaten at the ashram in the morning and stopped for water at several places along the way; that was all.

I walked and walked along the highway that goes to Delhi and beyond, passing through Mohibullapur, Bhithauli, Bakshi-ka-Talab, Sarainya, and Arjunpur, until it was evening and I finally neared Itaunja. I had walked about 32 kilometres, was exhausted, and it was getting late. I stopped at Turki village near Itaunja and spent the night with a distant relative there. The next morning, I began walking again, and finally reached Deora early in the morning. Everyone was surprised to see me that early but I did not divulge the entire story.

I returned to Lucknow in the third week of June, when the results of the high-school exam were normally declared. I stayed in a school managed by the family of a friend in Katara, Abuturab Khan, in old Lucknow. Around midnight, newspaper hawkers began shouting that the results had been announced and special editions printed. I kept sleeping as everyone rushed out to buy copies of the papers, those who passed returning in jovial spirits. The ruckus finally woke me, but I thought I would go out and get my own copy after the initial frenzy had died down.

Then a student rushed in and told me frantically: 'Shiva Balak, your name is not on the list!' That meant that I had failed! I jumped the *charpai* in a panic and rushed to see the results. I found my name among the first divisioners; my friend had overlooked that section completely and scanned only the second-division list.

By July 1956, it was time to sign up for intermediate studies (Class 12) and choose subjects from amongst the biology and mathematics groups. The biology teacher was trying to persuade me to join his stream. I had got the highest marks in the college in biology, and it would have been the logical choice, but the spectre of my poor drawing skills was haunting me. I decided against it and opted for the mathematics group.

By this time I had become confident among city boys and was familiar with different parts of Lucknow. I was becoming more aware of what was happening around me too, having access to newspapers in the library. I realized how much was happening around us in the country.

It was 1957, free India's second election; and my first. That election was also the first for a certain Atal Behari Vajpayee. He would go on to be prime minister twice at the turn of the century, a full four decades later. Back then, he was just a young man with the ability to fire up crowds with moving speeches about Hindi, Hindu, and Hindustan.

When he lost the election, it broke our hearts. Of course, the fledgling Jana Sangh to which he belonged had no chance against the Congress in the national election. The Jana Sangh was just six years old, born in 1951, just in time for free India's first election the following year. The Congress had been around for over seventy-two years, had led the freedom struggle from the front, and had Jawaharlal Nehru.

Our campus was becoming increasing politically conscious. There was a student agitation in Lucknow University against the then chief minister Chandra Bhanu Gupta, the education minister Jugal Kishore, and the governor K.M. Munshi, after a medical student, Gayandar, had died in a police baton charge. Although the student union was apolitical, the leaders were generally socialist.

To show our solidarity, we also assembled in our college ground and were about to leave the campus to join the strike, when Pandit Shridhar Singh, our principal, came up to us and asked: 'What is the matter?' He had a grand personality, wore a *sherwani* and pyjamas, and everyone, even the teachers, held him in respectful awe.

When he was told about the university students' strike, he declared, 'Our students do not go on strike'. He did not shout or express any outrage, but all the students returned to their classes. He was a kind-hearted and reasonable man, our principal. I remember the occasion when the payment of my scholarship, awarded to me for my ranking on the merit list of the Uttar Pradesh Board, was delayed. I was afraid to go to his room, so I wrote an application, starting with: '*Ka varsha jab krishi sukhane* (What good are rains when crops have dried up)', and then narrated the story of the delay in the payment of my scholarship. He ensured I got the money in three days. When it arrived, I couldn't believe it. I had Rs 112 in my hands; more money than I had ever seen before.

The very next day, I went to my village with the money. During the 12 kilometre walk from Itaunja to Deora, I counted the money at least three times, stopping at culverts at Mahona, Asanaha, and Atesua. I knew the tally would be the same, but I could not resist taking it out and counting it.

I gave every penny to my father, to enable him to repay some of the loans he had taken to support my studies. It may not sound much now, but it was a princely sum in 1957. Rs 112 could buy 15 grammes of gold, valued at over Rs 30,000 today.

I recently visited the home of Ravi Shanker, my college friend, and asked him what he had done with his scholarship money. 'Wait!' he said, and disappeared into another room. He emerged after a while with a very old watch. He had gone to Aminabad with his father, he told me, and bought the greatly prized 'Romer Popular' watch for Rs 105 and had also bought a gold-tipped Swan pen for seven rupees. He preserved the pen till he joined the Geological Survey of India (that's probably his way of saying he lost it thereafter) and treasures the watch to this day.

In an attempt to earn some extra pocket money that summer, I became a hawker for a day, selling newspapers announcing the results of the UP Board exam. I had the curious notion that on result day one could earn good money as papers bought by hawkers for 50 paise each were sold for up to Rs 3 each. I bought 50 newspapers and covered many lanes and bylanes of Lucknow trying to sell them, but I was late and got no customers.

Losing patience, and wanting to at least recover my principal amount, I went to the Aminabad main crossing and started shouting: 'Result in fifty paise! Result in fifty paise!' The regular hawkers got angry and one of them came to me and said: 'How many papers do you have?' I said, 'Twenty'.

'Give them all to me and take this money,' he snapped. I handed over the papers, took the ten rupees and never again tried to make a quick buck.

at a crossroads, a little blue mark

I had never owned a watch, never combed my hair under an electric bulb, and I could not speak or understand English properly. Each of these handicaps would haunt me in my first weeks at Lucknow University, that sprawling idyll of learning of which I was so proud to be a part.

My educational career was constrained by several considerations. I had closed the option of becoming a doctor when I left biology in my Intermediate classes and I was not financially in a position to think of engineering as a career. I had no compulsion to take up a small job so I decided to go in for higher studies at Lucknow University.

In so many ways, the man I would become was determined by Lucknow University. I sometimes look back with wonder: How did I hurtle blindly through so many pivotal moments and yet somehow made the right choices? Isn't life after all just a series of crossroads? You can only see that far down, and all too often, we aren't even looking. It was in just such a blind rush that I chose geology.

I was filling out the admission forms for a bachelor's degree in science. My main subjects would be physics and mathematics, but the options for the others were mind-boggling, especially to me, the teen from Deora who had only ever owned two textbooks all through school.

Standing with my pen in hand at the registrar's office, I was trying to complete the admission form when I came to the dreaded multiple-choice: chemistry, geology, statistics, or astronomy. Some of my friends had purchased admission forms in advance and had come to submit them. They must have had a discussion about the pros and cons of choosing one or the other optional subject. For my part, I had no real idea of what any of it meant. I therefore looked over at my friends' forms and saw they were all ticking the box beside geology. Without a second thought, I ticked it too.

That little blue mark, so thoughtlessly made, would shape the rest of my life, my entire career, and steer me in the direction of the rest of my story. When I think about it, I still feel actual pangs of fear that so much should have been at stake and I had not even known it. What if I had opted for statistics instead? Would I be crunching away numbers in a government office? What then if I had opted for astronomy? Would I have been peering into a massive telescope in some lonely planetarium? In any event, I chose geology, and I have never had any regrets.

It was July 1958: humid and sweltering. The departments of geology, physics, and mathematics were about 200 metres away from each other and there was no bell to indicate the end of each class.

I didn't have a watch, so I blindly followed my classmates who, I figured, had a better idea of the time. We used to walk in a group from one department to the other, talking, laughing, and gossiping as we walked. Most classes in geology appeared to be fun. Dr S.B. Bhatia, who moved to the University of Chandigarh sometime later, was a wonderful teacher. Another popular teacher was K.S. Valdiya, a migrant from Burma (Myanmar). My favourite teacher was, however, Professor

R.C. Misra, a stout, fair-complexioned, well-dressed man who was head of the department of geology and made rocks seem so fascinating.

I stayed in touch with Professor Misra for decades, meeting him every now and again. He always greeted me with the same warmth. The professor and his wife had no children, and recently died a lonely death after living stoically for decades in a desolate mansion in a posh area of Lucknow.

English was the first obstacle I faced in the B.Sc. first year course, and resolved to meet it head-on. Although quite shy, I forced myself to ask the teachers to be kind enough to explain what they were saying in Hindi. This request was never turned down, but their Hindi was not exactly of the highest quality. Many of the sentences they used in fact contained English terms and Hindi grammar and I had to stifle giggles at sentences such as 'Igneous rock *ki jo* character *hai, sabse* strong *banati hain* (The character of igneous rock makes it the strongest).' The General English class, though only a qualifying subject at the graduation level, gradually improved my spoken English. I was now reading an English newspaper every day: the *Hindustan Times*. In an uncanny coincidence, exactly fifty years after I began reading that paper, my son became the deputy executive editor of it.

So many crossroads, so many intersections!

* * *

I was enjoying college, but it wasn't easy: even for the professors. There was so much to get done, and there never seemed to be sufficient time! On one occasion, Dr J.P. Jaiswal was teaching us Mathematics and got so carried away that he did not realize his half hour was up. As a signal, many students began scraping their shoes on the floor, producing a loud scratching sound. Dr Jaiswal was furious and roared, 'You are scratching the ground now; you will scratch your heads later!' He was right. He set very tough questions in the terminal test and all but a few students failed. The marks of the terminal tests were added to those of the final examination, so it was fortunate that Ravi Shanker and I made it through. He had passed, I had just about scraped through.

Dr Nigam's classes in optics were another hurdle. It's hard to understand light when you've never seen a bulb! I still remember my first practicals in optics. Dr Nigam asked me, 'If you were combing your hair, would you focus the light on your face or on the mirror?' I had no idea. I had always combed my hair in sunlight! Hesitantly, I muttered: 'mirror.' The professor probably understood why I had answered incorrectly. He patiently explained that the object, not the mirror, should be illuminated.

The final examinations for B.Sc. took only about a week, starting on Monday and finishing on Saturday. The B.Sc. first year exams were only qualifiers so that was fine. However, in the second year, revising two years' notes all night and writing the exam in the morning was a tough task. I used to take a medicine, which I think was called methedine, to keep awake all night. One day, I heard that my senior in Government Jubilee Inter-College, Roop Kishan Das, a medical student, had collapsed because he had stayed up all night throughout the MBBS exams. I thereafter stopped taking pills to keep awake.

My B.Sc. results broke my heart. It was the first time I had slipped to the second division. I decided I would make up for this in the M.Sc. exam. Oddly, the subject I had chosen on a whim proved to be the one most likely to help me get a job. Geologists were in great demand, and I decided that geology would be the subject for the master's.

I studied hard, attended every lecture, and was indeed so diligent that it upset some of my classmates. The students in my class would occasionally skip lectures en masse. They would fix the date in advance, make their own plans with their friends, and just not turn up. If no one turned up, the class would automatically be deemed cancelled. I would defy them every time and attend the classes.

Therefore, if the lecturer walked in, marked me present and the rest absent, we would then nod politely to one another and go our separate ways. I, often to the library, the professor, presumably, for a well-earned cup of tea.

One of my classmates, I.P. Srivastava, the class bully, adopted the technique of (what we now call) 'Gandhigiri' to deal with my obstinate behaviour. He came up to me on campus one day and lay prostrate on the floor in front of me. I was so embarrassed that I pleaded with him to get back on his feet. He got up and said, 'Panditji (that is what they used to call me, because I studied all the time, 'like a learned priest',), when you go to the class and your attendance is marked, the day is counted. The teacher takes attendance and goes away without teaching you. You do not gain anything, but we lose,' he said. In those days, 75 per cent attendance was compulsory or you could not take the final exams. 'What should I do?' I asked. 'Please cooperate with the class,' he said. I nodded my approval ... I had to because I was afraid he would lie down again and embarrass me.

Such abstentions were however few and far between. The university campus was generally peaceful, free from violence and vandalism. Student leaders respected teachers, the books, and the campus. I generally kept away from their noisy gatherings, meetings, and agitations, but sometimes I would peep over the heads from the back of the crowd to see what was going on.

I remember one student union president speaking at the Canning College quadrangle, saying even policemen in plainclothes were not allowed at the meeting. 'I urge the policemen to leave the meeting ground,' he said. Some people did leave the venue. The unions were quite powerful, and they knew it.

Jagdish Gandhi, president of the Lucknow University Students' Union (who now owns a huge chain of schools), once called for a strike to force the removal of Professor Kali Prasad, head of the psychology department. The allegations against Professor Prasad related to moral turpitude. Gandhi was a strict moralist and was known to practice what he preached. He was also a popular president.

In response to his call, a mammoth procession walked from the university through the Vidhan Sabha (the state secretariat) towards Lucknow railway station. I had joined the procession out of curiosity, not knowing why it was heading towards the station. The destination had apparently been the local police station. Once there, an altercation broke out. I was far behind and could not see what was happening. Suddenly, shots were fired. I bolted, dashed into a nearby house, and sat there till calm was restored. Thankfully, the family living there did not chase me away and kindly let me stay till things calmed down.

Some thirteen years had passed since Independence by now, but the resentment against symbols of British colonial rule still simmered. There were agitations seeking the removal of old statues of Britishers at prominent places and against the continued use of the English language in government offices. The youth wing of the Socialist Party of Dr Ram Manohar Lohia painted most of the statues black. Queen Victoria's statue near the General Post Office (GPO) in Hazaratganj was among the first to be removed and was replaced by a statue of Mahatma Gandhi.

I think the winter of 1960 was the coldest in decades. The entire city seemed to grind to a halt. Schools and colleges were closed and people sat around whatever little fires they could keep alight. We were a group of eight friends staying together, with just the bare minimum: an almirah for each of us in a wall in the veranda, free of rent but no bed.

Unable to buy firewood, we had no option other then to remain under our blankets for most of the day. The fact that our bedding was on the floor only added to our woes. It was so cold that we hired a short, stocky male cook (who had a bulging belly and sparkling teeth) to run the common kitchen. Even this thick-skinned chap had a really tough time during the chilly winter.

Many of my friends were facing problems of their own. One of my juniors, Jagat Narain of Atesua village, had failed a couple of times and was worried he would fail the Intermediate examination. In the meantime he had gone to Aminabad to listen to a lecture by Atal Behari Vajpayee. He decided to give up his studies and join the armed forces instead. He went to the recruitment office in Sadar, Lucknow, got through, and was enlisted as a sepoy clerk. He retired a few years ago as ammunition inspector (subedar), he told me recently. Another friend, Sahdeo Awasthi, who was studying for the B.Com exam, got into a fix over a love interest. Sahdeo was related to Bacchu Maharaj, who looked after security and the general upkeep at the ghats of the Gomti where we lived and also rented out boats. Bacchu Maharaj had asked Sahdeo to tutor his only daughter, who was in high school. The two fell in love and wanted to marry. Sahdeo's maternal uncle, his guardian, was, however, very reluctant. He felt the whole arrangement was a trap.

There was quite a lot of tension even after the two wed. But eventually it all settled down.

I, meanwhile, was going through some medical horrors. I had developed lumbago (pain in the hip joint) and had been admitted to the students' ward of Lucknow Medical College for treatment under Dr B.N. Sinha, a renowned orthopaedic doctor. His technique was quite bizarre. He fixed a hard wooden strip along my side from shoulder to ankle to make me immobile. I felt like Jesus Christ on the cross.

One day I felt an acute pain in my knee joint and removed the wooden strip. When the junior doctors, who were terrified of Dr Sinha, saw what I had done, they rushed me in a wheelchair to his office. Dr Sinha was so furious with me that his eyes seemed to start out of their sockets and he yelled: 'This is treatment, not *tamasha*!' I did not say anything, but he continued to rant: 'I will report the matter to the proctor!' Finally I replied, meekly: 'But sir, I cannot bear the pain.'

Soon after, R.D. Sharma, who had been my mathematics teacher in Government Jubilee Inter-College visited me in the ward and suggested I consult Dr A. Ghosh, a renowned homeopath in Lucknow. By this time, I had been at the hospital for thirty-eight days. I finally left against medical advice.

The homeopath gave me a syrup to take every half hour by the clock. At 8 p.m. on the first day, my knee began moving for the first time in a month and a half. In a week, I was back to normal.

I decided to pay my previous doctors a visit. I walked in, absolutely fine, all the young doctors staring at me as if they were seeing the ghost of the poor soul they had thought would never walk again. I had recuperated in time to save my academic year and retain my grades.

On my next visit to Dr Ghosh, I recognized one of the patients: one of the interns from the medical college. He was there to get himself treated for a boil-like growth in the cheek!

* * *

I was not in favour of watching movies and my classmates knew it. They used to tease me: 'Unless you see a movie, how can you say it has a bad effect?'

S.B. Misra with his wife Nirmala. This picture was taken a few months after their wedding.

Two sons (twins) Neelesh (right) and Shailesh (left) of S.B. Misra and Nirmala, during their winter vacation in school in Nainital.

S.B. Misra and Nirmala during their wedding ceremony on 14 May 1972.

Some of S.B. Misra's childhood teachers: Sharda Baksh Singh (sitting in centre in garland), Brahmadin (sitting extreme left), Bhim Singh (sitting second from left) and Syam Nandan Misra (sitting third from left).

S.B. Misra with his sons Neelesh (right) and Shailesh (left).

The first teacher of Bharatiya Gramin Vidyalaya, Kunaura Shripal (extreme left), S.B. Misra's step-brother Gangadhar (second from right) and Shripal's sister Ranno, a student in the first batch.

Co-educational Junior High School started by S.B. Misra and Nirmala at Kunaura in 1972. Rampati (extreme right) and Mishri Lal (third from extreme left) were among the first to take admission in the school.

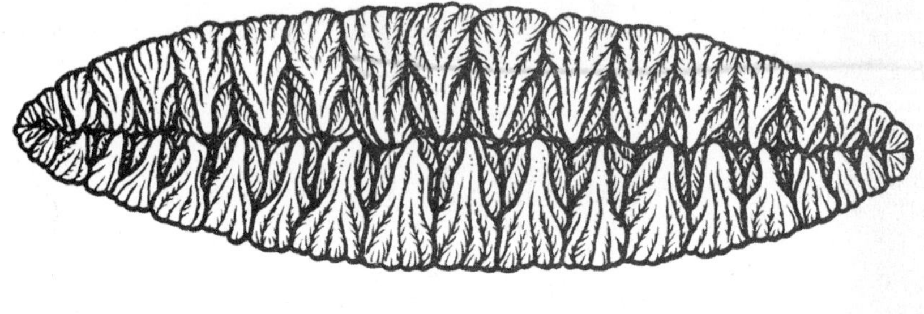

10 cm

ETYMOLOGY: The genus name is a compound of the Latin words *fractus* meaning "broken" or "fractured", being the source of "fractal", and *fusus* meaning "spindle". The species name honours S. B. Misra who, as a graduate student, first drew attention to these fossils at Mistaken Point in 1967.

Spindle-shaped animal named after S.B. Misra as *Fractofusus misrai* and explained in its etymology. (Courtesy G.M. Narbonne)

565-million-years-old fossils from Mistaken Point area in the Avalon Peninsula of Newfoundland, Canada.

Rugged eastern part of the Avalon Peninsula of Newfoundland in S.B. Misra's thesis area, with the rocks forming a huge coastal anticline.

S.B. Misra with his friends Nirankar Prasad (right) and K.K.Singh (left) near Niagara Falls (on Canadian side) when they took Misra there to cheer him up.

S.B. Misra in his childhood school at Itaunja.

Dr Adam Gilmore, a senior space scientist from NASA explaining a satellite model to the students of Bharatiya Gramin Vidyalaya, Kunaura after his lecture in the school campus. (Photo by Pankaj Jaiswal of HT).

Students of Bharatiya Gramin Vidyalaya, Kunaura taking examination sitting on the ground.

Karan Dalal (standing in background) from Mumbai who recently joined the Bharatiya Gramin Vidyalaya school project, after leaving a lucrative job, to teach computer science to rural students.

Governor of Uttar Pradesh Shri T. Rajeswar (left) felicitating S.B. Misra and Nirmala Misra (Photo courtesy Pankaj Sah of the *Times of India*).

Neelesh Misra (extreme left) sitting on stairs, his twin brother Shailesh with wife Aditi (extreme right). Neelesh is 18 minutes elder to Shailesh.

I can proudly say that they were not able to change my mind, until other friends did some years later, and (I have to admit with some embarrassment) I did a complete U-turn and became crazy about films! Now my son writes lyrics for Bollywood songs with titles like 'Jadu Hai Nasha Hai', and I must admit they are catchy. Well ... what can you say, *zamaana badal gaya hai* (times have changed).

Back then, my friend Ravi Shankar was also not fond of movies. Friends like Dhiraj Banerjee, Surendra Kumar, and Anupam Misra, though serious students, used to argue that we should at least watch good Hindi films (the word 'Bollywood' was yet to be coined) like *Jhanak Jhanak Payal Baje, Do Bigha Zamin, Kagaz ke Phool,* and the likes, but they never skipped classes to go and watch films.

Far away from Bollywood, we lived in the real world and its cruel realities periodically jolted us. In 1961, we had devastating floods when the Gomti river breached its banks. The one-storey building at Rastogi Ghat where we were living was nearly submerged. Bacchu Maharaj's boats were busy rescuing people all day. We had shifted to the terrace above the first floor, where we had to live for about a week. One of those days, a corpse came floating by and got wedged along the outside wall of the terrace. We were uncomfortable all night but no one wanted to touch it or go too close lest its ghost terrify us later. By morning, it had been swept away by the swirling currents.

I completed the M.Sc. (geology) exam in April 1962, but the stress had taken a severe toll on my health. I had become quite weak and weighed less than fifty kilograms. I needed some rest, so I decided to go back to Deora for the summer vacation.

It was great to be home, where I didn't have to count the pennies or cook my own food. Everyone wanted to hear tales of the big city and all I was studying. The air was fresh and soon I felt revived. However, throughout the summer, like a record stuck in one groove, the nagging worry about the results continued. In June, the results were out and I returned to Lucknow. I had vindicated myself and was one of only four students to get first division. The test by fire was, however, about to begin. It was time to find a job.

a village boy becomes a teacher

One afternoon, R.D. Sharma, the mathematics teacher who had saved me from the incompetent doctors, paid me a surprise visit. It was a very touching gesture. He was one of the teachers who really cared about his students. He asked me whether I would take up a job as assistant teacher in the chemistry department at Jubilee Inter-College. I had distinction marks in chemistry in the Intermediate but I had not taken it at degree level.

I was initially reluctant, as the job had nothing to do with geology and I was eager to get my career going. On the other hand, I needed money, so I allowed myself be persuaded and accepted the offer. In July 1962, I joined the college in L.T. Grade at a basic salary of Rs 120 a month. For someone who had been earning Rs 25 a month taking tuitions, it was a fortune. I decided to give myself a complete makeover as a special treat to celebrate my new wealth. First, I went to a tailor and ordered myself two new white shirts and two pairs of trousers, my favourite combination: white shirt and white trousers!

It was a strange and exhilarating feeling. Less than four years after I had signed up there as a goofy student, I was a teacher at Government Jubilee Inter-College. I felt very awkward: several of my old teachers, like M.N. Sinha, Mr Khare (whose first name I do not remember) and R.D. Sharma, who had taught me English, physics, and maths, were now suddenly my colleagues. While they were very kind and quickly welcomed their recently graduated student as a peer, I took time to get used to the new situation.

It was during this period that I filled out an application form for a job at the Oil and Natural Gas Commission. In August 1962, I was called for an interview. Some of my friends, including Ravi Shanker, Anupam Misra, and Avinash Chandra, had already joined ONGC, which had been carved out of the Geological Survey of India in 1957. The commission was recruiting geologists in large numbers.

In September 1962, I received an offer from ONGC to join as technical assistant. I had to report at the headquarters at Dehradun, in what is now Uttarakhand. I felt quite guilty at leaving the college mid-session, but the principal, B.D. Dixit, advised me to accept the offer, as it was better than the grade in which I was working. 'If you receive a better offer, leave ONGC too,' he said, adding that quitting jobs would never be seen as a flaw. 'One can even quit the governorship,' he concluded.

While I was preparing for a career in science and readying myself for my trip to Dehradun, some people in my village suggested that I become a *vakil* (lawyer) because I could grow in the company of several good lawyers from Kumbhrawan, a nearby village. My father did not express an opinion as he had acknowledged that I was a better judge in such matters. He was satisfied even with the salary I had been getting as assistant teacher.

I therefore decided for myself. In the last week of September, I boarded the Doon Express. My train pulled into Dehradun the following morning. I do not remember if I had made a reservation but there were no crowds in the trains then. I got a room at Komal Hotel, where my friends were already staying.

Not very far from Dehradun, along the border with China, tensions were growing. After years of supposedly great relations, the sheen of 'Hindi-Chini Bhai Bhai (Indians and Chinese as brothers)' was wearing thin and sporadic Chinese intrusions were reported in north and north-east India.

China had refused to recognize the McMahon Line as a boundary between the two countries. Newspaper reports said our defence minister, V.K. Krishna Menon, had neglected our borders and 'allowed the manufacture of coffee percolators rather than weapons in ordinance factories'. War broke out between India and China on 20 October 1962. Nehruji felt betrayed by China and Menon was caught napping. A few weeks earlier he had been delivering a lecture in the United Nations that the fear of China was exaggerated. The people of India felt humiliated. The city of Dehradun lived in constant fear of what the battle at its doorstep would bring. If there were fears in the real world, my friends wanted me to escape to the make-believe world that I had resisted for so long: the movies.

My argument for avoiding movies during my student days no longer held any water, they said. Finally, they virtually dragged me to the cinema hall for my first film ever. It turned out to be *The Guns of Navarone.* From my remote, primitive village with the threat of no education at all to watching a Hollywood film, I had certainly come a long, long way! I was overwhelmed by the movie, but I remember asking my friends why they were depicting romance in a war film. The love scenes confused me, but they marked the beginning of the end of my aversion to films. We switched genres the next day and went to see *Tarzan*.

* * *

ONGC, my employer, was expanding fast. Exploration was in full swing in the Ankleswar oil fields of Gujarat. Most of us were transferred from Dehradun to Gujarat after about a month. I was unaware of the turbulence: North Indians versus south Indians, geologists versus chemists and drillers.

Two of my classmates from Lucknow, Nirankar Prasad and Shailendra Saxena, were also posted at Bharuch near Baroda, assigned to work with the drilling rigs. The three of us rented a big house in Bharuch and hired a lady cook. There was just one problem: she put sugar in the *daal* (lentils), a pivotal part of every Indian meal. We therefore politely inquired whether she had made a mistake, to which she crisply responded: 'It will not taste good if there is no sugar.' That was their way in Gujarat: sugar in the *daal*. Therefore every so often, to assuage the trauma of the sweet *daal*, we would eat spicy *chaat* and seek solace in the movies.

Bharuch had only one cinema hall in 1963, and each movie would run for weeks, sometimes months. That wasn't good enough for us movie freaks. We just couldn't wait that long. We were willing to go the distance to catch the latest film, even if that distance happened to be 100 kilometres.

Nirankar, Shailendra, and I took train rides of up to a 100 kilometres to the towns of Surat and Baroda just to watch movies on weekends. We had to time it very carefully so as not to miss the start of our show. It didn't matter which movie was playing; it just had to be a new one. In just a year we saw scores of movies, sometimes three a day! [Shailendra Saxena had shifted to the Geological Survey of India and served there for many decades. He died some years ago. Nirankar Prasad went to Canada and settled there as a Canadian citizen.]

After the war with China broke out, cinema owners would play the national anthem at the end of each screening. Everyone was supposed to stand in silence as a sign of respect, but few did. Many, especially the children, would walk about. Others would keep talking, some even remained sitting. This was annoying, and we thought the practice of playing the national anthem in this way was not right. I have seen the trend continue to this day and the attitude of the audience remains the same.

I especially remember a few films from that time, like *Mother India* and *Rustam aur Sohrab*. A film called *Anpadh* (Illiterate) had particularly appealed to me because it dealt with the issues of illiteracy in rural India.

Gujarat had a vibrant spirit of its own. Women in large numbers would perform the traditional *garba* dance in the open and we would sometimes go to watch as they swished gracefully in their multicoloured garments. On Makar Sankranti (14 January), the festival that marks the winter solstice, there would be hundreds of kites in the skies of Baroda and Bharuch. People of all religions spoke fluent Gujarati, ate the same food, and were all peace-loving. This was, after all, the land of Gandhi. I liked Gujarat, its people, and culture. It was here that I got an opportunity to interact with foreigners for the first time.

There were two Russian experts in our division, V.I. Kuzmin and V.V. Denisov from Moscow. I was closer to Denisov. They were not as forthcoming and outspoken as we Indians. Once I asked Denisov: 'Why did Khrushchev get the coffin of Stalin removed from the Kremlin graveyard?' He simply said, 'Stalin was right for his time and Khrushchev is right for now.' The Russians were very proud of their country. The Russian equipment was crudely made and difficult to handle in comparison to its American counterpart, but the Russians would always praise the tools made in their country.

In the winter of 1963, I was transferred to the north-eastern part of India, to Sibsagar in Assam. I had no complaints because, to a village boy who had not seen anything of the country, it was exciting to travel and, in any case, I knew no difference between Gujarat and Assam.

A few days before I was scheduled to leave Bharuch, V.V. Denisov organized a farewell dinner at his house. It was a wonderful gesture on his part and a special honour for me. He lived in Ankleswar, about 50 kilometres from Bharuch, where I lived. I travelled to his house for the party and was warmly greeted.

To my horror, I had forgotten to tell him that I was a strict vegetarian. Before me, on their massive dining table, was a lavish spread such as I could never have imagined, really couldn't have imagined being in the same room with so many dead animals. Spread before me were various types of fish, chicken, and heaven knows what other slaughtered animals. When I told Denisov I could not eat any of the dishes, he was very disappointed and I was terribly embarrassed. I picked at some bread, butter and salad and had some coffee. It was a lesson I never forgot: always, always tell your host what you eat.

I left for my new assignment in Sibsagar, travelling in a first-class train compartment for the first time in my life. The journey to Sibsagar in Assam via Mugalsarai in UP and Barauni in Bihar was the longest I had ever taken, and this north-eastern part of India might just as well have been another planet. Villagers in Assam told all sorts of crazy stories about sex and witchcraft. The belief in the villages was that women transformed men into sheep and goats and kept them in their possession for as long as they wished. When I had gone home briefly before taking up my new assignment, my father had said: 'Don't go that far if you don't want to.' I had laughed off his apprehensions, and here I was in a land of witches and cursed goats. I had hardly any expenses, however, and was happy that I would be able to send home some money. I sent home a telegram saying I had reached safely, and that telegram took a week to get to Deora.

Letters took about a fortnight in those days. Replies from my father were drafted by Janki Prasad, the village headman, because my father was hesitant to write in his own hand. There was no privacy of communication in those days. His letters would provide information about the family and the village, and about his financial condition and requirements, all told word by word to the headman. In my letters, I would describe the town, send money through postal money orders, and write about my well-being.

Once, I had gone to the market in the evening and asked a little girl in Assamese what her name was. She replied in a sweet voice 'Aapni Akhami Aahe'. What a pretty name, I thought. I realized only much later that she had replied: Are you Assamese? I always intended to learn the Assamese language, but it never happened. In ONGC, there was no public dealing and I did not have contact with any Assamese family. Employees in the office spoke either in English or Hindi. I was therefore only able to speak a smattering of Assamese.

Across the border in East Pakistan (now Bangladesh), a new crisis was brewing. There was bloodshed in Dhaka and other areas and reports of communal riots were pouring in. My mind was agitated but there was nothing I or anyone in Sibsagar could do. I let off some steam by writing a poem against the democratic government of India, which was not speaking out against the riots. One of the lines of the poem I had written was: '*Bharat Maa ke adhkhile phool, Tibbat ki murjhai kaliyan, is prajatantra se poochh rahin Dhaka ki khoon bhari galiyan*' (What about the half-blossomed flowers of Mother India, dried up buds of Tibet, the blood soaked lanes of Dhaka are questioning this democracy). I used to compose such poems now and then to express my feelings and that was all. Before going to Canada, I had recited the poems to my landlady in Lucknow. She had taken copies of the poems but I do not know what happened to them.

The people of Assam had faced many difficulties during the Chinese aggression the previous year. Illiteracy, unemployment, and poverty were causing widespread resentment too. A strong resentment was therefore developing against outsiders, particularly Bengalis, and the Assamese wanted them out. The Assamese resented the fact that the Bengalis, being more educated, were grabbing all the jobs. The province had not been divided into the smaller states of Arunachal Pradesh, Meghalaya, and Manipur at the time and local aspirations were raising their heads. Despite all this, the situation was more peaceful than it is today.

In May 1964, I had gone on work to my old office in Bharuch when a Gujarati Muslim driver who knew me from my earlier days there approached me with a gloomy face, almost in tears, and said: 'Sir, Nehruji *khallas ho gaye* (Sir, Nehruji is dead).' He had heard it on the radio. I was stunned because I had read in the newspapers that Nehruji, our first prime minister and the architect of modern India, was in Bhubaneswar at a Congress Working Committee meeting.

I rushed into the office and saw my colleagues sitting frozen in their chairs. No one felt like working any longer. We left the building and saw our grief reflected in every face on the street. The anger and hard feelings that had developed against the government during the Chinese aggression and the humiliation of the country by the Chinese melted away.

There was no TV then. We stayed glued to our radios all day and read all the stories in the newspapers the next day. The common man was as worried as the politicians, wondering: 'After Nehru, who ... what?' Senior Congress leader Kamraj Nadar had the answer. In the name of consensus, he sidelined Morarji Desai and gave India a prime minister in Lal Bahadur Shastri, a Nehruvian who would go on to become a darling of the masses.

A few days later, I returned to Sibsagar and resumed work. Several colleagues were sending applications to foreign universities for higher studies. I also sent a few applications, including one to Memorial University in Newfoundland, Canada. Although a foreign degree or going abroad was not part of my tangible ambitions, I said to myself: 'You never know ...'

I wasn't happy at work, lacking job satisfaction. I dreamt of becoming a good teacher. I was becoming restless and homesick. I had a lot of earned leave piled up, and one day I encashed some of the leave, got a first-class ticket (to which I was now entitled) and left for home without a tangible plan in mind.

I did not get a reservation, despite that first-class ticket, because I had refused to bribe the clerk at the booking counter or the railway conductor in the train. I had therefore to travel in an unreserved, jam-packed, third-class compartment car for the sixty hours to Lucknow with a first-class ticket in my pocket.

I had packed all my belongings in a large sized tin trunk, as if to shift permanently.

* * *

I had always wanted a job in Lucknow. Incidentally, a position for the head of department in geology had been advertised at Kanya Kubja Degree College (now Jai Narain Degree College) some time earlier and the last date for application was still a few days away. I submitted my application for the post and wanted to attend the interview before returning to Sibsagar. God was kind: I got the job and was back in my city, in a prestigious position and making decent money. Life seemed set, or so I imagined.

I was happier as a teacher than I had ever been at ONGC. Mine was a single-teacher department, and I had a peon named Sitaram to assist me. He was a lean, dark, short young man. He would always arrive early and wait in front of the department till I came in at 10 a.m. I didn't make him come to my house to collect the keys in the mornings or drop them off in the evenings as the other heads of departments did because Sitaram lived in Charbagh, which was far away from where I lived. [About four decades later, Sitaram was still at the college. I went there to conduct the practical exams and he greeted me with a smiling face.]

There were 20 students in the department then. They had all listed geology as their second option, their first being chemistry. Denied admission in the latter, they had ended up in my class. The spacious department and laboratory did not interest them. It was a challenge to inspire indifferent students and to convince the management of the necessity of rocks, minerals, and fossil samples as part of the teaching programme.

Initially, the college manager, Jai Narain Misra, was himself unwilling to sanction money for field trips, important for training geology students and collecting samples. He later relented and sanctioned money for a trip to Rajasthan. On the trip, the students collected colourful mineral samples and rocks, and began getting drawn to the subject. Many of the samples went into our department museum.

We had completed our field trip through five towns in Rajasthan and planned a three-day stay at Kishengarh during the return journey. When we got there, however, a state-level sports competition was on and all the hotels and *dharamshalas* (spiritual hostels) were full. We had no place to stay, so I went to Dr Chatterjee, a medical doctor who often helped geological groups from Lucknow University and elsewhere. He said there was a vacant *dharamshala*, but it had been locked up for over a decade. 'If you are brave enough to stay there, I can get it opened up for you,' he said. We had no option but to accept whatever was available. He arranged for it to be cleaned, and handed the keys to us. All of us had carried our own bedding and, after tea and snacks in the market, we turned in for the night. I was about to turn in myself in my small dusty room when one of my students, U.K. Shrivastava, knocked on my door. 'What's the matter?' I asked him. He came in and sat down. I thought he had come with a complaint about some student. He was very tense, almost trembling, his face pale, and his voice shaking. I tried to calm him down and find out what was wrong but he could barely speak. 'Are you all right, Umesh?' I asked. 'I have been here before,' he said. 'So what?' I replied.

Normally, a meaningless exchange like this would have annoyed me, but the boy seemed petrified. 'What's bothering you, Umesh?' I asked. 'There is a door at the back of the building,' he replied. 'I was murdered here. I tried to run from the back door ... I was chased and killed.'

A chill ran down my spine. The boy was obviously serious. He had remembered something from his previous life. I called two of the most sincere boys in the class and asked them to take Umesh with them and sleep alongside him. The next morning, he seemed all right and I wondered whether I had perhaps taken a frightened boy's fantastic tale too seriously.

The expressions on people's faces in the market the following morning changed my mind. As we walked out of the hostel, people stared and whispered. No one had used the building, an old man said, since a wedding ended in tragedy there ten years ago. There had apparently been some dispute, he whispered, and the bride had jumped into the well. It was just outside the back door. Hadn't I seen it?

* * *

I took the same group of students to Bihar for field training and brought back a huge collection of minerals, rocks, and plant fossils that I then arranged on tables for labelling. Professor R.C. Misra of Lucknow University visited our college soon after and came to our department. He asked Kakaji (that is how he was addressed), the sceptical manager: 'How much do you think these samples are worth?' When the manager did not reply, Prof. Misra snapped: 'They must be worth at least Rs 10,000!' Thereafter, all my proposals for field trips were promptly sanctioned and funded.

By the following year, in July 1965, the number of students in my class had doubled, and geology was their first choice. They were also more energetic than the earlier batch, organizing several exhibitions and lectures. This was during the first Indo–Pak war and the students, in collaboration with their other classmates, organized a grand cultural programme in Ravindralaya and collected substantial money to be sent to the defence fund through our principal.

In early 1966, I became serious about starting a school in my village to fulfill my childhood dream. The first step in this direction was the formation of a registered society, the Gram Sudhar Samiti Karuwa (Committee to Improve the Village of Karuwa). Beecham of Mohan Meakin was the president, P.L. Bali, the vice-president, and I the manager. The committee had two other members, Janki Prasad, the village headman, and one of my students, Banshi Dhar Chhablani.

Back at the college, I took my second batch of forty students on a long tour up to Tiruchirapally and Madras fossil areas. I remember the guide in Tiruchirapally had said, 'Sir you are looking for stones that are *shota shota, gol gol* (shmall-shmall, round-round)'. I had said, 'Yes, yes', and he had taken us to an area where we found a huge reserve of fossils about 160-million-years old! Within two years, the museum of the department was full of precious samples collected by my students and I. Decades later, I visited the department as an external examiner and was proud to see that many of our samples were still there.

During this tour in 1966, I had gone to the Madras railway station to buy tickets for the students and myself. I handed over the concession forms to the booking clerk and said, 'Ticket *bana deejiye*' (Please issue our tickets). The man, it seems, had just been waiting to hear a Hindi word from us northerners. Like a tiger pouncing on its prey, he shouted: 'Don't you know Tamil?' I said I didn't. He growled back: 'Can't you learn?' As I fumbled, he issued the tickets with a stern warning: 'Learn Tamil.'

The entire state of Madras (now Tamil Nadu) was boiling with anger under the leadership of Ramaswamy Naicker against what they thought was the imposition of Hindi. The slogan of 'Hindi, Hindu, Hindustan' by the then Jana Sangh had been reverberating in the air for quite a while in north India. English signboards were being painted black by Socialist Party workers and the reaction of the booking clerk represented the other side of the coin.

It was a difficult time, not because of the war against Pakistan but because of the war against hunger and poverty. Lal Bahadur Shastri, our prime minister, had framed the slogan 'Jai Jawan, Jai Kisan (Hail the Soldier, Hail the Farmer)' and asked the people to grow wheat on their lawns and in their gardens. He also asked people to refrain from eating on Monday evenings. The entire city, indeed, the entire country, observed the fasts at his call, such was the moral authority and influence he exercised over the common man.

During the war with Pakistan in 1965, the Indian forces had demolished the reputation of the Patton tanks in the Khem Karan sector. I remember once hearing Prime Minister Shastriji talk at Aminuddaula Park. He said: 'Ayub Saheb [then the Pakistani president] was saying we will have dinner in Delhi. We thought let us have lunch in Lahore.' Indeed, the Indian armed forces were said to have reached the outskirts of Lahore. Shastriji's statement drew thunderous applause.

After a ceasefire, brokered by the United Nations, the Russian government under Khrushchev invited the Pakistani president Ayub Khan and Shastriji to Tashkent for talks. Many people in India thought Shastriji should not go. He went, and we heard over the radio and read in the newspapers that the pact was signed on 10 January 1966.

On 11 January I was taking a bath at my new rented home, owned by one of my students, Vimal Shrivastava. Vimal came rushing to my room and called out for me, shouting: 'Sir, sir! Shastriji *nahin rahe* (Shastriji is no more)'. I wrapped the towel around my waist and rushed out of the bathroom. 'I have heard on the radio, sir!' he said, weeping. We looked at each other. It was as if one of our own had died. We could not eat that day.

A few months later, I moved in with my younger stepbrother Gangadhar, whom I had helped get admission to Class 9 at Government Jubilee Inter-College.

My life seemed to be looking up, but there was always the nagging guilt: I had not yet set up the village school of my dreams. One of the initial hurdles was the unavailability of land. Our ancestral land was only three acres, barely sufficient to support the family, and I did not have sufficient money to buy any more.

While passing through Mahona village on my bicycle, I would see a fat man with a huge belly walking about. Lala Panna Lal Rastogi was a moneylender from Lucknow. He often travelled to my village, lending money. Panna Lal was always accompanied by two musclemen, one carrying a bundle of his registers, the other, a big lathi with a sharp steel tip at one end. Rastogi would write Rs 100 in the register and give only Rs 90, the rest being *likhai* (writing charges). The borrower had to pay back Rs 10 every month for 12 months. The rate of interest thus compounded came to about 80 per cent. This was a little less than what Moghalias (Pathans) charged the farmers, so some were actually grateful. There was however no way I could borrow from him.

While I had the school on my mind, there were other things to deal with too. Proposals for marriage were coming in fast and thick, and I no longer had any excuse to say 'No'. One of the proposals came with a fat dowry and a house in Barabanki. Another came for the daughter of a certain Kali Datta Shukla, head of the political science department at Kanya Kubja Degree College where I was teaching. Our principal, Vidya Ram Misra, was taking a personal interest in this one. I was inclined to say yes, but before the matter could be taken any further, my life would go through a 360-degree turn.

One afternoon in April 1966, I was relaxing after lectures when I saw a well-built man walking to my rooms with an envelope in his hand. As he drew closer I recognized Devendra Kumar Shrivastava, a former colleague of mine at ONGC in Sibsagar, Assam. He had come on earned leave, just as I had two years ago, and had brought with him a letter that had come for me in Sibsagar.

It was another one of those crossroads that would transform my life. If my former colleague had not been kind enough to bring my letter from the town hundreds of kilometres away, I would probably never have known of it. My life would have been completely different.

It was my little window to the future, all wrapped up in paper. I opened the envelope and read the letter. It was from Professor W.D. Brueckner, chairman of the geology department of Memorial University in St John's, Newfoundland, offering admission, scholarship, and airfare from Lucknow to St John's in Canada. I was required to join the university in October 1966.

(first) flight of my life

I had never imagined, as I filled out the application forms in Assam, that I would get a scholarship to a foreign university. Now I was going to step on an airplane; become only the second person I knew to ever leave the country (the first being a very distant relative).

I had to race against time, arranging for a passport, visa, and foreign exchange, and await the air ticket. Could it be that they would really send me an air ticket, I wondered. What if it didn't come, I fretted, sometimes staying up all night at the horror of the thought. I wouldn't fly; wouldn't study abroad. It seemed more plausible to me that it would all fall through than that I would actually board a giant metal bird and travel to a foreign country at the other end of the earth. There were worries too. I had no idea of Newfoundland; no idea of anywhere abroad. What would I eat in Canada? What would I wear?

All I knew was what I had been taught in the geography class: that the Gulf Stream, carrying hot water, and the Labrador current, carrying cold water, meet in the Atlantic Ocean to create the most favourable conditions for the breeding of fish and growth of the fishing industry.

I knew of one person who had gone abroad for studies, K.P. Misra of Tikra village, 5 kilometre from Deora. He had gone to Washington DC on a government scholarship. He gave me some guidance about the paperwork to be completed. I was very concerned about what I should wear there, for I would be representing India on several occasions, a number of my friends told me.

To me, India meant the land of Lal Bahadur Shastri, who had become very popular in those days, so I thought I should take a dhoti, kurta, and Gandhi cap with me, I also packed a small copy of the Ramayana and the Bhagvad Gita.

Professor R.C. Misra, my geology professor from Lucknow University, signed as my guarantor and the Regional Passport Office issued a passport to me on 20 June 1966. It was then a most impressive looking document, with the seal of our nation printed in gold on the cover. I still have that first passport.

With my passport in hand, I needed a visa for which I had to pass a medical test by the doctor prescribed by the High Commission of Canada in New Delhi, and then I would be all set. I would travel in October 1966. I went to New Delhi and consulted the prescribed doctor. He found me fit in all respects barring tiny worms called *Taenia nana* in the stool. I had to get rid of them. The tiny creatures appeared to present a serious stumbling block. Time was running out and I was getting nervous. I returned to Lucknow, consulted Dr N.N. Gupta of Lucknow Medical College and the *Taenia* were eliminated. I went back to New Delhi, obtained the doctor's clearance, and got the visa from the Canadian immigration officer on 26 August 1966, valid up to 30 September. There appeared to be a ray of hope after the shadow cast by the *Taenia*.

Canada was in the hard currency area in those days and one Canadian dollar was worth Rs 7. I had obtained permission from the Reserve Bank of India, Kanpur, to get 200 Canadian dollars against, as I remember, Rs 1400. I bought a small black suitcase from Nazirabad and packed my white dhoti, kurta, the Bhagvad Gita and Ramayana, and a few warm clothes. [I eventually brought the suitcase back from Canada and kept it for decades.]

I now had a passport, visa, foreign currency, and received an air ticket from Lucknow to St John's through a travel agency in early September 1966. The flight from Lucknow to Delhi was scheduled for some time in the last week of September. However, the suspense was still not over. I was informed by the Air India people that no flight was available to me from New Delhi on or before 30 September, the last date of validity of my visa. I had to get the validity extended until 20 October.

Dr Ramesh Gupta, a colleague from Kanya Kubja Degree College, had given me some *tuar daal* (yellow lentils) and a bottle of pickle to be delivered to a certain Dr Sanwal, a vet in Ottawa. Apparently, he had no idea of the distance between St John's and Ottawa – 1,774 kilometres – and nor did I. As for me, I did not take any edibles for myself.

On my last day at the college, my students in the geology department of K.K. Degree College arranged a farewell party and gave me several gifts, including a beautifully carved *rehal* or stand for an open book. On it was a citation eulogizing my association with them. Their affection and regard touched me deeply. The following day, I went to meet my friend Ravi Shanker. His mother anointed me with a *tilak* and blessed me when I left their house.

From Lucknow to New Delhi I was to travel by Indian Airlines, our state-run domestic airline; from New Delhi to London, I would fly Air India, the state-run international airline, and from there onwards it would be Canadian Airlines. The village headman Janki Prasad Misra and my father had come to Lucknow airport to see me off. I said goodbye to everyone at Rastogi Ghat, where I used to live when I was a student, and went to the office of Indian Airlines in Lucknow. Here I was informed that the connecting flight from Delhi to London was not available on that day. I was asked to start on 4 October, in the afternoon, from the domestic airport a short distance away. Airlines in India were completely under the control of government then. There was no competition, and flights were randomly cancelled and invariably delayed.

For my little group of well-wishers, the change in dates was a terrible disappointment. The village headman and my father returned to the village and I vended my way back to Rastogi Ghat where I spent an anxious, aimless week. I began wishing I had consulted a pundit for the *mahurat* (auspicious time) before finalizing my departure. Enough seemed to be going wrong and I would have liked to have the stars on my side.

Soon it was 4 October and time to head to Amausi airport, Lucknow's domestic terminal. The airport was deserted. There were no real security risks then, so the checks were cursory. When my plane finally took off, there were only two people there to see me off: my father and Lachhman Bajpai, the youngest son of Shiva Govind Bajpai, the grand old man of Deora. In those days, relatives were allowed to accompany passengers all the way in up to a viewing gallery that looked out right on to the runway. My father and Lachhman watched as I climbed the ladder into the plane.

I felt so proud. I was off on a grand adventure, just like the young men from the pages of fiction. I imagined my father with tears in his eyes as he watched his eldest child fly off. What stories they would tell back in the village, I thought, of the first plane to ever actually be seen, and climbed into, by someone from Deora. I was still sceptical about the trip because of its apparently inauspicious beginning.

When I reached Delhi in the evening, there was still no Air India flight available. In that age of monopoly, there was no one to complain to. I found out when the next one was likely to leave and checked into a hotel. Fortunately, I had some Indian currency with me and I could pay for a few nights in Delhi. On the morning of 6 October, I took an Air India bus from their Connaught Place office in the heart of the capital to Palam airport. I exchanged the Indian currency I had left for five Canadian dollars and boarded the plane on 6 October 1966, this time with no one to see me off.

This was a much larger plane than that for the domestic flight and I was relatively comfortable. During take-off, I felt a little nauseous, but was not otherwise at all afraid. The plane took off and, in a few hours, we were flying over the mighty Himalayas.

The plane would take a longer route, via Moscow, because the route via Pakistan was not open to India after the Indo–Pak war the previous year. As we flew, the flight crew told us which peaks we were crossing, the altitude, and other details.

After crossing the grasslands of the Steppes, the plane flew over the tall coniferous forests of the Taiga, and it was like seeing my geography textbook of days gone by gradually come alive. I was fascinated by the view, having never before been more than two storeys above the ground, and here I was watching hills, trees, and clouds glide by thousands of feet below me.

Then came the announcement: 'We are about to land at Moscow airport. Passengers are advised to put on warm clothes.' There was bright sunshine outside and I thought it amusing that they should want us to swaddle up. I went out in just what I was wearing and, goodness, the temperature outside was seven degrees celsius. I couldn't stop shivering. All my warm clothes were in my luggage in the plane, so I just rushed with the others into the centrally heated airport where it was quite comfortable.

At the airport, I could see the warmth of the Indo–Russian friendship that I had read about in the newspapers. The announcements were made in Russian which I did not comprehend, but I didn't need to understand Russian to appreciate the friendly gestures from the Russians. We were offered tea, coffee, and snacks with great respect, and all of us were treated as honoured guests. Although I was no admirer of the socialist economy, I had always appreciated their respect for Indian languages, tradition, and culture. A few years ago, a Russian delegation had visited Kanpur where they were welcomed in the English language. To the utter surprise of the hosts, they had replied in Hindi. The terminal was impressive, with clean floors, fresh air, and smiling faces greeting the passengers. Outside the airport we could see tall conifer trees all around.

It was my first step into the unknown. I had never seen so many white faces before, and women were walking hand-in-hand with men right there in the airport. Many of them did not even look married. Unusual, to say the least.

After my association with Kuzmin and Denisov, the greetings like '*Dobrautra*' (Hello) and '*Drastuvite*' (Good Morning) were familiar, but the Russians greeted us with something even more familiar: '*Namaste*'. I felt like staying a little longer but it was time for our plane to take off. A few members of the airport staff bade us goodbye. I do not remember the type of bus or the mode of transport to the Air India plane but I do remember '*Paiyakhali*' (let us move). We went straight to the plane.

Our next stop was at the Heathrow airport in London, where I had to change from Air India to Canadian Airlines, with a wait of a few hours. The airport building at London was much more crowded than anything I had seen or imagined. Planes were taking off all the time, some even hovering overhead, awaiting their turn to land on the crowded runways.

Women in *salwar-kameezes* were cleaning the floor of the building. I felt humiliated and thought to myself, 'Is this what they come here for?' It did not matter to me whether they were Indians or Pakistanis. They were our people, and they were still slaves of the British.

At Heathrow, there were more white men and women, hugging and kissing, moving unhesitatingly hand-in-hand. Unimaginable to me! In rural India, women were nameless, usually referred to as 'Ramu *ki maa*' (Ramu's mother) or 'Gajodhar *ki dulhan*' (Gajodhar's bride), and invariably walking a few paces behind the men, and were never so much as touched in public even by their husbands.

On the Indian flights, food had been no problem. They had offered very good quality vegetarian meals. Now however, as I began the next leg of my journey, I began worrying: What would I eat? The options were confined to boiled vegetables, soup, and juices, bread, milk, and rice pudding. I thought I could easily survive on these on the flight, as well as in Canada. I was conscious that my spoken English might amuse the British so I might not be able to converse freely. For my part, I paid special attention when speaking to them, and could sense the formality of their behaviour as opposed to the warmth of the Russians at Moscow.

During the halt at Heathrow airport, I had neither the time nor the inclination to leave the airport, and perhaps I would not have been permitted to do so. Anyhow, I was content to spend the time watching people, or the luggage emerging on the conveyor belts, and thinking about the Indians in this part of the world. Most of the time I was only physically present at the airport, my mind was in Newfoundland.

I sent a telegram from Heathrow to the chairman of the geology department of Memorial University, and boarded the plane for Canada on the evening of 6 October. The plane, flying over the Atlantic Ocean at night, took me to the airport at Montreal, where in the early hours of 7 October the authorities stamped my passport 'Non-Immigrant entered'. Then came another flight, my fourth in 24 hours, from Montreal to St John's. I eventually landed at St John's airport, Newfoundland, at 9 o'clock on the morning of 7 October, fatigued and, by now, extremely nervous. I was unaware of what jetlag was, so I felt more disoriented than I could explain. I thought of Deora, and Uttar Pradesh. Even fancy Lucknow seemed homely and familiar now.

St John's, I would later learn, was the oldest city in North America. The airport was smaller even than that in Moscow, yet it was very impressive. There was bright sunshine outside and it was pleasantly warm, with an autumn breeze. I would soon discover that such weather was a rarity in Newfoundland. People waited for the rare days when they got to say: 'Nice weather, isn't it?' The people here spoke more about the weather than anything else.

I looked around. The people at the airport were interacting very little among themselves and making no noise at all. I was among white men who looked like the Englishmen who had ruled India for centuries. It was a strange feeling. I reminded myself: 'I have come here to learn from them.' I picked my one small, black suitcase off the conveyor belt and set it down on the ground beside me. It was then that I realized, with a rush of terror, that I had no idea how to reach Memorial University. I did not even have the telephone number of Professor Brueckner, the chairman of the geology department, with whom I had been corresponding.

I rummaged through my case desperately, looking for the admission papers. I found them, and, fortunately, the paper bore a phone number. I headed to the nearest public phone booth and was about to lift the receiver when I saw a robust elderly man with a glowing face striding towards me. 'S.B. Misra?' he asked. 'Yes, sir,' I said loudly. 'Brueckner,' he whispered, and held out his hand. [Note to self: these people are really soft-spoken.]

I shook hands with Professor Brueckner and felt honoured. The research supervisor and head of department had come all the way to the airport to receive a mere graduate. Imagine that. I felt like touching his feet, as was the custom when greeting elders and teachers back home, but I knew that this was not a form of greeting used in this part of the world. I expressed profuse thanks and gratitude, and he led me to his car parked outside the airport.

That's when I got my second surprise: Professor Brueckner would be driving us himself. This would have been unthinkable in India. The head of every department I could think of in Lucknow University had always sat in the back seat, directing the chauffeur every now and then as he relaxed against the cushions. In later years, I would see Joseph Robert Smallwood, the premier of Newfoundland and Labrador, driving himself about, without any bodyguards, without any cars following him with screeching sirens, as was the norm in India.

As we drove out of the airport, Professor Brueckner asked: 'You didn't bring your wife?' Oh dear, I thought, time for this conversation again. 'Sir,' I said, in the usual semi-apologetic tone, 'I am not married'. Indeed, I had asked Prof. Brueckner in one of my letters from Lucknow, if I could bring my wife in case I got married in the meantime. He had agreed, so my marital status or lack of it was a matter of surprise for him.

As Professor Brueckner drove, I realized how different everything looked around me. The area near the airport had hardly any homes. There seemed to be no people here at all. There were a few bushes, but no cattle. Not a single cow on the road, and none even by the roadside. We had some limited conversation on the way, especially about my job back home. He knew I had one. I explained that as I had been unable to secure study leave I had resigned from my job.

Professor Brueckner drove straight to the hostel and arranged for my stay in a two-room suite. He had asked someone to help me with admissions at the Dean's office and I completed all the formalities that very day. I had imagined that all the hostel rooms were like the one I was in, and I was telling a fellow Indian, Mukut Bihari Bajpai, doing research in chemistry, during lunch that the rooms were better even than in the pictures I had seen in magazines back home, when he laughed and said the suite was just temporary. He was right. In a week, I was shifted to Room 426, Hatcher House, but the regular room was also self-contained, with a double bed, a table, and table lamps!

I thought of Deora, and all the many dark villages of my country, where students had no space to study; where the more fortunate had the dim light of a lantern and a jute bag to spread on the ground. I thought back to how I had studied on a jute mat in the failing light, after walking 24 kilometres. I thanked whatever greater power had guided me to make all the choices that had led me here, and I swore to take the fullest advantage of this opportunity. That very day I also promised myself that I would build a school in my village which would have electric lights; a place where children from far away could come whether they were in a position to pay for their books or not; where they would be free to study as long as they wished ... until nightfall if they chose.

The Memorial University of Newfoundland (MUN) was a relatively new university, created out of Memorial University College (MUS) in 1949 by the Government of Newfoundland, headed by Joseph Robert Smallwood, who was the premier of the province. When I joined the university in 1966, it had just moved to its new address and had four principal buildings: education, science and engineering, arts and administration. The administrative set-up was efficient and responsive. Every student had easy access to the dean of faculty; the staff of the faculty office were polite and helpful. How different it was from the Dean's office in Lucknow University where the peon at the door had to obtain permission before allowing someone to enter.

The Indian community in St John's was confined mostly to the university and consisted of about 100 people. Among the research students, there was my roommate Somyajulu, a geophysics student from Andhra Pradesh; physics student H. Sanjeeviah of Manasgangotri, Mysore University, in Karnataka; Lagu from Maharashtra, who was studying mathematics; Chandrashekhar from Andhra Pradesh, studying zoology; and a girl called Sheela Lobo from the Konkan region of Maharashtra. In the Arts faculty I can remember a certain Ram in the history department who belonged to Karnataka but came from Kenya where he had been teaching.

Among the seniors, Dr S.P. Reddy from Andhra Pradesh was a popular teacher in the Physics department and there was another teacher, Ricchhaiya, not so popular, in the same department. A certain Dr Kunduri Viswasunder Rao was working as a post-doctoral fellow. There were several students from West Pakistan, including Shamim Ahmad; Mohd Azam, a Khatri from West Pakistan; Mohd Karamat Ali in the physics department from East Pakistan who used to tell me in private conversations about the discrimination against Bengalis in East Pakistan (now Bangladesh). His views, emotional sometimes, were a sample of simmering discontent and I cannot imagine what might have happened to him after his return to Dhaka University then. I had read in the newspapers that the soldiers of Gen. Niazi of East Pakistan had killed most intellectuals, particularly of Dhaka University. Notwithstanding the recent Indo–Pak war, and the quarrels over languages and state borders within India, we nurtured no prejudices towards one another here on foreign soil.

The geology department, though small, was truly international, with students from South Korea, China, Formosa (now Taiwan), Ceylon (now Sri Lanka), and England, besides India, Pakistan, and Canada.

Food was, however, definitely a problem. The cafeteria in the campus always had plenty of juices, milk, soup, boiled vegetables, and fruits, yet the smell of meat and eggs was all-pervasive and nauseating to me.

The Indian students from different departments would meet during lunch and dinner, and have endless discussions about food. We would talk about our favourite dishes back home, and wonder how any people could go through life chewing on the strange-looking vegetables and meat preparations we saw around us. Another thing that bewildered us were the timings of the meals. Breakfast and lunch, though a little early, were manageable. Dinner was, however, early in the evening, and we would always get hungry again at night. We would invariably keep cake, bread, apples, and dry fruit in the drawer of our bedside tables as insurance.

H. Sanjeeviah and I were the only vegetarian students and were well and truly miserable in terms of food. Some of my new friends had been trying for a while to convince me that eggs didn't count as non-vegetarian fare. About that time, a certain Puri, a strict vegetarian from India living in Bell Island nearby, had a paralytic stroke, which rumour had it had been caused by lack of animal protein. I don't know if it was the scare that the rumour caused or sheer exhaustion from the lack of choices, but I began eating eggs, and have to admit that breakfast was a great deal more fun from then on.

St John's, located on the east coast of Canada, was the capital of the province of Newfoundland and Labrador. It had a well-developed harbour, an airport, a railway station, and most other facilities of a modern city. I saw a centrally heated train for the first time when I went to see a friend off to mainland Canada (that is how they called it then). Back home we had not till then introduced air-conditioned trains, or if we had I was not aware of them. After the train journey in Newfoundland, he would catch a ferry to mainland Canada. The province of Newfoundland and Labrador, with only one university and no major industries apart from fisheries, was lagging behind the other states of Canada. Nevertheless, there were pre-university colleges in every town of the province. The people were simple and honest, but they hated being called 'Newfis', a nickname foisted on them by the rest of the country. They also hated their state being called Newfoundland rather than 'Newfinland'. I felt they should have spelt it differently, if that's how they felt about it.

a not-so mistaken point

I had always thought of the white man as wealthy, well-educated, even pampered. It therefore came as quite a shock to me that one of my own teachers had made it to Newfoundland against considerable odds, much as I had. Dr V.S. Papezik had fled Czechoslovakia during the Russian invasion and worked in the mines of Canada for several years, saving up money, a few dollars at a time, to enable him to complete his university education. He was a very sincere teacher and an inspiration to me. Most of the teachers at Memorial University were extremely nice.

I still remember Professor H.J. Hughes, who would bring apples and nuts as a special treat for me every day. This was a little embarrassing and I asked him not to do so. He promptly stopped bringing me the treats, but I have thought in later years that I should perhaps have been more sensitive to the feelings of the ageing gentleman. He had no children of his own and had obviously become quite fond of the polite village boy from faraway India. If I had it to do over again, I would just have swallowed the jibes from my friends and accepted the apples with grace.

My studies were progressing well at the university, but the weather was dreadful. It was foggy and damp in summer, and windy and freezing in winter. There was central heating at St John's and oil furnaces kept the houses warm in the towns. In the more remote areas, the wooden homes were heated by beautifully carved fireplaces with blazing logs. Many students went skating and skiing in the winter. I was reluctant to step outside, into the howling wind and snowfall, so I spent my time in the library or studied in my room.

Professor Brueckner had given me a master key for my room, the departmental library, and the laboratories, so I could study at any time, day or night. It was not a special gesture, but a regular facility afforded to all research students.

In the biting cold, we would go to the department late at night through tunnels connecting the buildings underground, and work as long as we liked. Many Indian and some foreign students worked even on the weekends.

My social life in Newfoundland was limited to gatherings of Indian students and cultural programmes during festivals and on other important occasions. The library was one place where boys and girls of different departments would meet and get acquainted. The cafeteria was the other. The whites seemed to do precious little studying here, and quite a lot of the getting acquainted. I remember one morning sitting in the cafeteria having a cup of coffee when a student asked if he could join me. I said, 'Sure, be seated'. A few minutes later, his friend Margaret Walsh came and joined us. They were undergraduate students who I had often run into in the library.

A few evenings later, Margaret met me in the cafeteria with another young man. We had coffee together before going to the library, and I remember being very surprised to find her roaming around with a second young man just days after I had seen her with the first. I soon learned that that was how they did things here. The girls went out with different boys, in a sort of trial and error process, till they found one with whom they wanted to settle down.

They, particularly girls, began this process of trial and error as teens and got frustrated if they could not be 'steady' by their early twenties. Back home, finding a groom for a girl was the parents' responsibility. Arranged marriages, I was told, had earlier also been common in Europe.

Like many others in Newfoundland, and perhaps throughout Canada, the young university students had wild misconceptions about India. Once they got to know me a bit, they often wanted to know if all they had heard was true. 'Mr Misra,' Margaret once asked me, 'is it true that people travel on elephants in India?' I laughingly explained that a bicycle was more than most could afford, and elephants would have been highly impracticable on our busy streets.

Study and research at the geology department of Memorial University was divided into two parts: theory, to be completed in the winters, and a thesis based on field or laboratory studies, generally completed in the summer. For the thesis project, I was allotted the geological mapping of the southern part of the Avalon Peninsula of Newfoundland. This was a very remote area and no Canadian student wanted the assignment. The rough and remote areas were usually allotted to foreign students. Thus, Chitra Ket Singh was alotted Hodgewater Group, Avinash Nautiyal was alotted Bell Island, Seok Koh the Trepassey area, and I was alotted Mistaken Point.

In April 1967, soon after the winter ended, examinations were held for the theory component. I was well prepared and wrote my exams with confidence. Then it was time to think about the thesis work, which consisted of geological mapping, laboratory studies, and writing the actual thesis. Professor Brueckner asked if I would accept the challenge of mapping the south-eastern part of the Avalon Peninsula, the Mistaken Point area. I agreed with slight reservations, because fellow students had told me the area was inhabited by huge wild animals like the moose, caribou, and wild bears. 'They will kill you,' I had been told quite sombrely; 'just claw you apart with their huge paws and eat you alive'.

When I told Professor Brueckner of these stories, he laughed and said, 'Misra, it is a virgin, unmapped area and you can make discoveries there'. That caught my attention. Although I knew that a fellow Indian student a few years my senior had declined the area and opted for Bell Island, I accepted. It's a good thing I didn't let myself be discouraged or I might have taken the wrong path, because, although I had no inkling of it then, this was another crossroad for me.

Mistaken Point was about 150 kilometres from St John's, near Biscay Bay, and you could go all the way there by taxi; so much for wild animals and dense forests. It was, however, remote and isolated, with no more than 2,000 people living there along a deserted and bleak 40-kilometre stretch of coastline.

The topography sheet suggested that there were only three settlements in the area: Portugal Cove South, Biscay Bay, and Cape Race, with populations of 350, 76, and 3 families, respectively.

Professor Brueckner had appointed an undergraduate student, Donald J. Fitzpatrick, to assist me in the field. Don, as we called him, stayed at Portugal Cove South with me in a boarding house run by Hanna Coombs, an affectionate elderly lady.

I think I caused Mrs Coombs some consternation. She had asked me, soon after I arrived, what I would like for my meals. When I told her I was a vegetarian, she said, 'No problem, you must be eating pullets'. I replied in the negative. What about fish, she asked curiously. When I again replied in the negative, she seemed quite disappointed and very confused and said, 'My gosh, what am I going to feed you?'

Mrs Coombs, bless her, did her best, offering me rice pudding, boiled vegetables, a few pieces of homemade bread, and a glass of milk for dinner. For lunch, she would pack bread, butter, and coke, which I would supplement with a few bars of chocolate to enable me to make it through the day.

Don used to drive me around in his car every day, from Portugal Cove South to different parts of the area. He remained with me for most of the field season. At Portugal Cove South they made their own cream and bread, used wood stoves and oil furnaces, and played card games like poker and 'Crazy Eight' to while away the time.

There was no industry, apart from one fish processing plant along the coast. The children would follow me with friendly curiosity, probably fascinated to see someone of a different colour. They however never came too close, made any comments, or disturbed us in any way. The nearby town of Trepassey was a hub of activity for the area and the people there were hospitable, friendly, and compassionate. It had two reasonably large churches, two schools, department stores, recreation centres for weekly dances, and playgrounds. The department store, which supplied groceries and other items of daily use to the surrounding areas, obtained its stocks from St John's.

Each week, in the afternoon, there would be a game of jackpot, involving considerable skill and luck. Pretty much the entire population of Trepassey and Portugal Cove South would assemble in the hall for the game and there was much excitement and laughter over every number called. The jackpot game was played by a mixed gathering comprising teenagers, adults, and the elderly. It was a kind of weekly get-together. In the evening, in the same hall, there would be community entertainment involving music and dance. A majority of young boys and girls at such get-togethers were on the lookout for a partner. People like me just sat on a bench, drinking Coke and watching the goings on. I felt very grown up and was above age. More than that, however, there was a college teacher sitting inside me. How would I invite a girl for a dance even if I was able to overcome my shyness. I remained reserved but there was no racial inhibition. Everyone considered me highly qualified as a university education was a rare thing in that remote area. I simply could not adapt to the social norms.

I was told that the area was fairly backward by North American standards in the 1960s, but had come a long way since the 1940s. Apparently, radio, indoor plumbing, and electricity had only arrived twenty years before I did.

Meanwhile, I had my work cut out for me. The area to be mapped was a 25-mile stretch of coastline of continuous rock covered inland by loose soil or glacial debris. At twenty-six, I was full of energy and ideas, but the job at hand was quite tough, and the hours very long. Work began early in the morning and we were on our feet till evening. The bread-

and-butter diet was telling on my health and I realized I would have to adapt to Canadian ways of eating. It was difficult to even imagine giving up my vegetarianism, but the only option was to quit and return home. I finally asked my landlady to gradually introduce animal protein into my meals, starting with chicken soup, fish, and pullets in that order.

For them I was still a vegetarian, because I did not eat the meat of large animals. I tried to tell myself that, given that I was in Canada now, surely I was as vegetarian as one could be there. Deep down, however, I was aware that I had lost something; an essential part of who I was, or rather, who I had been. I felt I had betrayed my Brahmin ancestors. I also dreaded meeting a chicken, lest it look at me with accusation writ large in its beady eyes.

I was however physically fitter to work now, and as I worked I noticed that the rocks, like the pages of a book, held hidden records embedded in them. For the first time I interpreted the role of turbidity current, such as mud flows on the ocean floor, in the deposition of rocks in the Mistaken Point area. My interpretation of the direction of ancient currents also suggested that the land mass of the Avalon Peninsula was once a deep marine trench. For the first time, I distinguished the types of rocks in the Mistaken Point area and also coined the term 'Drook Formation', among others, and got it registered with the Department of Interiors. To this day, I have the letter of acknowledgement sent to me on 15 January 1970 by Robert G. Bates, then secretary of the Geologic Names Committee in the United States Department of Interiors, Washington DC.

I feel a sense of pride that every geological interpretation I made some forty years ago has stood the test of time: the relative chronology of the rock sequence, conditions at the ocean bottom where the rocks were once soft sediments, turbidity currents, direction of flow of sediments at the Precambrian ocean bottom, sliding soft sediments as slump structures, volcanism, and above all the Precambrian fossils that have now been dated by others to be 565-million-years old.

Hank Williams and A.F. King later mapped a large chunk of the Avalon Peninsula in the mid-1970s and retained most of my conclusions in the report of their study submitted to the Geological Survey of Canada. Every geological conclusion I made in the Mistaken Point area was a first.

Back at Portugal Cove South, it was time for Don to return to St John's, but I still needed a car. He therefore volunteered to teach me to drive and suggested I buy his automobile. I readily agreed, because I had no other alternative.

One day, he was taking me on a test drive when I ran over a dog and fractured two of its legs. I was horrified at having caused the animal such agony and began apologizing profusely to the owner of the dog. That gentleman had, meanwhile, ducked into his home and returned with a gun. I thought that threatening to shoot us was a bit extreme, especially as it was he who had let his dog out on to the street without a leash. Then I realized the gun was for the animal. The owner wanted Don to shoot the dog.

Don declined quite calmly, and they began discussing the legal angles of the matter. All this time, the dog was yelping in pain; its whimper so heart-breaking that it brought tears to my eyes. Finally, the owner let us go and I imagine he shot the animal soon after we left. It seemed so strange to me to kill a faithful animal just because it was hurt, rather than treat it.

I was afraid to drive after that, but eventually I got the hang of it. The test for a driver's licence at St John's was rigorous. First, there was a written exam about the traffic rules, signs, and all the rest, for which I had studied long and hard. That test proved to be a cakewalk. Then followed the practical test. The instructor asked me to drive down a slope. 'Stop,' he said mid-slope, and I dutifully halted the vehicle. 'Start,' he said a few seconds later. No problem there either. Then he asked me to take the vehicle up a slope. Mid-slope, he asked me to stop again, and when he asked me to start, the car wouldn't move. I became quite flustered and thought I had surely failed the test, but I made it through and bought my first car!

I now used to drive the car freely on the gravel road along the coastline in my field area. There were no population or grazing cattle to negotiate on the road; no threat of wild animals either. I also began taking the car to Trepassey during the weekends. I had a couple of mishaps on the way home from the weekly jackpot games, and I must say the police were generally very polite and helpful. My first crash was late on a Saturday evening. I was returning from Trepassey and visibility was very poor. The car skidded off the road and crashed into the side of a huge boulder. I tried to open the door on the driver's side, but it was stuck, so I had to clamber out through the other door and sat quite shaken for a while by the side of the road.

Within a few weeks, however, I became quite a confident motorist; in fact, on another drive back from Trepassey at night, I had an open road and pleasant weather and didn't even bother to see which side of the road I was driving on. A policeman followed me all the way home, then walked over and asked: 'Where do you think you are? In England?' I had been driving on the left all the while! I apologized quite profusely, but it took some convincing to reassure him that I wasn't drunk.

At around this time, Charles de Gaulle, then president of France, visited Canada. Relations between the British Canadians and French Canadians were not at all cordial at this time and the latter had been demanding separate statehood for the French-speaking provinces around Quebec. They even had a separatist slogan: 'Vive Quebec Libre (Long live a free Quebec)'. This had the seeds of two-nation theory with which we are familiar in India but the Canadians tackled the problem and averted partition of their country.

I used to tease my Canadian friends: 'You are so torn between two languages, but we have fourteen official languages, 500 dialects, and a dozen religions in India.' They were always startled at the extent of the diversity.

The area adjoining Trepassey had been assigned to my South Korean classmate, Seok Koh. He lived in the town for a while but shifted to Portugal Cove South with me after Don left because we both needed company, consultations, and discussions. We would accompany each other to the field area, each helping the other along. He had the habit of snoring and so did I. The problem was that whoever fell asleep first could really sleep at all! We often had long-drawn-out arguments about who snored louder and he would always end the argument by saying: 'Meesra, you don't know anyting' (with the emphasis on the 'ting' at the end). The truth is, he did snore louder and knew it.

Seok Koh suffered quite a tragedy while we were doing our theses. His fiancé of many years married another man back home in South Korea. When he found out, he had a protracted nervous breakdown and had to be admitted to an asylum at St John's. I visited him often after I returned from the field and he startled me the first time by saying, 'Listen to me, I am Jesus Christ'. Usually, he would just babble incoherently to himself. Professor Brueckner was father figure to all his students and he arranged for his proper medical treatment. Thankfully, Koh recovered in due course and completed his research programme. He went on to become a professor at the University of Seoul and eventually married and had two fine sons. We exchanged letters sometimes and he sent me a family photograph.

My field-work was progressing quite well. Back home, a rumour had spread about me: that I had died somewhere in the Canadian wild. Everyone in the village was crestfallen. There was no way of finding out more as they had no access to international calls. A week later, however, there was relief: my letter arrived in Deora. The rumour related to another Indian in Canada: Ram Narain Singh from Kasmanda in Sitapur district, and my classmate in Lucknow University, was caught in a snow-storm and died around the same time while engaged in geophysical investigation in British Columbia, the farthest western province of Canada. Ram Narain's story showcased how Indian students accepted challenges and staked their lives.

I was soon about to unwittingly do something similar. There was one afternoon at the Mistaken Point area that I will never forget. There had been a thick fog all day and I had been working alone on the cliffs along the coast. By now, I knew the place well. Mistaken Point had a surreal feel to it; I had heard stories of ships being wrecked here in the past. On that day, visibility was down to just a few feet and I was walking along when, suddenly, I looked ahead and realized there was nothing there. I was standing on the edge of a sheer drop, the Atlantic Ocean roaring on to the rocks several hundred feet below. I backed away cautiously and nearly collapsed on the wet grass. I returned home calmer, but I could hear that roar of the ocean for days.

a student becomes a discoverer

One afternoon in June 1967 I was tired and hungry so I sat down on a slab of rock at Mistaken Point for a snack. While I munched my sandwiches, I listened to the roar of the waves and gazed at the endless open ocean in front of me. I was getting back on my feet when I noticed some leaf-like imprints on the rock on which I had been sitting.

I decided to take a closer look and discovered clusters of intricately detailed imprints. 'They look just like fossils,' I thought. The imprints did not look like any fossil animals I had ever seen, and despite their leaf-like appearance, they couldn't possibly have been plants because these rocks had formed on the deep ocean floor.

These rocks were Precambrian, I knew. I also knew what that meant: the fossils, if that's what they were, would be no less than 500-million-years old. I told myself to slow down. 'If they're not organic, and prove to be just traces of mineral or metal, you will make a fool of yourself,' I thought. They didn't, however, look like traces of inorganic substances. They had once lived and breathed, in another time and in another environment, I argued in my mind.

In my mind, I heard Professor Brueckner's words: 'You can make discoveries there.' In an instant, I had forgotten the fatigue of the day's work. I studied the fossils as closely as I could in the dying light and took care to mark the spot so I could return. As dawn broke the next day, I sped back to Mistaken Point, my heart still racing, and driving quite fast. I was no wiser than the day before because I had no literature to consult and no one with whom to discuss my find. I however had daylight, and time on my side.

As I examined the rocks, I found a variety of forms. Many were leaf-like, but some were shaped like spindles, yet others had round bodies, and some looked like large jellyfish. The variety of forms eliminated the possibility of their being mechanical. The doubt had cleared and it was sheer excitement now. I still couldn't be certain whether these were the remains of plants or of animals, but I was sure they were organic, and I knew they were over 500-million-years old. I was a discoverer!

I worked for days without a break, barely bothering to eat as I took copious notes and several photographs of my find. It was agony when the sun set and I had to return to my lodgings. I would gladly have sat there all night, examining layer after layer of fossil-bearing rock.

All the fossils were covered with a few millimetres to about two centimetres of different-looking rock, which I later identified as volcanic tuff. At a later stage of my study I had got thin sections prepared for microscopic investigation and discussed it with Dr Papezik who had confirmed the covering rock was volcanic tuff. I wanted to collect many samples as I used to do in Kanya Kubja Degree College back home but that was not possible. The hard siliceous rocks containing fossils forming coastal cliffs were difficult to break. With great difficulty, I was able to collect four samples of the rock containing fossil impressions, which remain the only ones with any individual in the world. Not that others are not able to break the rock but the collection of fossils and breaking of rocks has been prohibited by the government of Newfoundland to protect the fossils. The area of my discovery is today an ecological park.

In July, I went to St John's with photographs of the fossils, sketches, using my poor drawing skills, and the four fossil-bearing rock samples. I was so proud that I couldn't wait to show my research supervisor, Professor Brueckner, what I had discovered.

We didn't, however, have any paleontologists in the department and I had no idea how to proceed. At the time, I didn't even know the exact age of the rocks I had been working on. They have since been dated by subsequent workers and found to be 565 million years old. Indeed, I became the first non-white in the world to have discovered fossils that old, and the first person to introduce Ediacaran Paleontology in the Geology Department of Memorial University.

During my stay at St John's, I made several visits to the central library and pored over publications on Precambrian life. There were only a few centres of study of such fossils in the world. In the journal *Science* I read an article by a Professor Martin F. Glaessner of the University of Adelaide, Australia, who was working on similar-looking fossils. I decided to write to him.

Prior to my discovery, there were reports of only a few Precambrian fossil occurrences in the whole of the north American continent, most of which were doubtful. However, in Australia R.C. Sprigg in 1947 had discovered such fossils from the Ediacara hills (hence the name Ediacaran fossils). Similar fossils were known also from Leicestershire in England and Trevor Ford was working on them. The other locality was Namibia, but the literature was mostly in the German language. Although many more fossils have been reported from different continents by geoscientists in the recent past, the Mistaken Point fossils remain to date the oldest and the best preserved.

Professor Brueckner had in the meanwhile visited my field area to verify my findings and was convinced that these were fossils. He was also happy at the progress I had made with my mapping and sedimentological study, except for one place near Cape Race. I had identified for the first time a major geological boundary between the older rocks of what was known as the Conception Group and the younger ones of the St John's Formation.

Professor Brueckner was not convinced about the demarcation. Suddenly, I realized why and said to him: 'Sir, on one side of the boundary are grey rocks and on the other side, purple ones. You are colour blind with regard to these two colours and that is why I am having difficulty in convincing you.' He laughed and agreed.

I had no idea at this point that Professor Brueckner was going on a year-long sabbatical. Before he left, however, he appointed Paul Thompson, a BSc student, as my field assistant to help me break rock samples and carry them for me. Paul was very serious, sober, and quiet. He remained with me until the end of the field season in September1967.

By now I had established that the rocks containing the fossils had been formed by turbidity currents like mud flows on the inclined ocean floor. I was also able to establish that the organisms, whether animals or plants, had died due to volcanism and been buried under a thin layer of volcanic tuff, much like what had happened to the ancient Roman city of Pompeii.

Recently, Professor A. Seilacher of Guebingen University in Germany referred to this in a reference to me in the dedication of his booklet *Fossil Art:* 'To Dr Misra, the discoverer of the Ediacaran Pompeii.' The analogy by Professor Seilacher refers to the Roman city near modern-day Naples, which has lain completely buried for hundreds of years after the catastrophic eruption of the volcanic Mount Vesuvius.

Back at Memorial University, Professor Brueckner went on his sabbatical in 1968 and M.M. Anderson, a Scottish gentleman, was appointed head of the department, bypassing the claims of all other faculty members who were PhD degree holders. Anderson had had a long association with Professor Brueckner, so perhaps that was why he was chosen, even though, as I later discovered, he only had a bachelor's degree.

I didn't really care about university politics. My only concern was my thesis. The field-work was complete and valuable information, including the discovery of Precambrian fossils, collated. All that remained was to write it out. Professor Brueckner, before he went on leave, had told me to work under Anderson's supervision. He was supposed to edit the chapters of my thesis, which he never did.

In the meantime I needed money to send home, not having been able to save much from the scholarship of $250 per month. In the summer of

1968, unaware of Anderson's designs, I took a job as a geologist with the Department of Mines, Government of Newfoundland and Labrador, to map part of the Avalon Peninsula, with John Mullins as party-in-charge. It was tough terrain, but Mullins was very appreciative of all my efforts. I still treasure a testimonial he gave me on 1 March 1974, on the completion of our project: 'Mr Misra worked with me through the four-month summer field season,' he said in the letter. 'He performed his duties, in what were often trying circumstances, in a highly competent manner. Mr Misra has a thorough knowledge of geological mapping techniques and is an excellent field geologist.'

Meanwhile, instead of editing the chapters of my thesis, as he was supposed to do, Anderson had used all my material to prepare a research note, and submitted it under his name in July 1968 to the research journal *Nature*, published from London.

He named me as the second author, as a sort of an aside, something I only discovered when I saw the piece in print. Like a true colonialist, Anderson had annexed my research material, using the power of his position and the absence of Professor Brueckner, to get away with this unethical act. I was heartbroken. The first public disclosure of all my hard work had gone under another name, that of someone who had had nothing to do with my discoveries. Anderson had never even been to the site when he wrote the paper. I was, however, aware of that but I could not take the matter up with Anderson because my scholarship money was paid through him. Indeed, Professor Brueckner, in a letter dated 30 July 1970, had written to me, in a different context, saying: 'Prof M.M. Anderson holds the strings of my research grant purses.' I never received any academic assistance from Anderson.

Indeed, Professor Papezik, who was my teacher during that time, once said, 'How can Anderson guide you? You are more qualified than he is.' I was surprised and asked what he meant? He said, 'Anderson does not even have an M.Sc. degree, which you have.' It was then that I discovered that Anderson had become a professor of geology on the strength of a B.Sc. (Hons) degree.

After the paper was published in *Nature*, Professor Goldring from Reading University in the UK was not convinced and wrote comments questioning the findings. Unabashed, Anderson asked me to draft a reply, which he then sent to the journal in his name, with mine, of course, mentioned again as an aside.

With Anderson busy annexing my work, my thesis was getting unduly delayed. I had realized by now that he had no interest in it, so I stopped showing the chapters to him. Elsewhere, the same work for which Anderson was trying to take credit was being credited to me by those with greater scruples. Professor Glaessner, the Australian who was working on similar-looking fossils in Adelaide, wrote to me on 7 November 1968, congratulating me on my discovery and asking me to send him casts of the fossils so that he could study them too. I sent him these by airmail and he made suggestions regarding the identification of the fossils, on the basis of which I assigned life forms to different groups of animals. Professor Glaessner was one of those who discussed my material in several publications, with due acknowledgement to me. He also wrote to me most kindly, saying I could quote the contents of his letter in my thesis.

With so many others quoting my work, and Anderson trying to grab credit for it, I decided to write a research paper of my own, without waiting for the completion of my thesis. I put all the details I had in the paper and submitted it in December 1968 to the *Geological Society of America Bulletin*.

After the publication of that paper in 1969, there was no room left for scepticism. The geological community the world over was convinced of the dating and authenticity of the fossils. Even Professor Goldring of Reading University, who had expressed doubts about the earlier paper, wrote to me on 30 December 1969, saying my paper in the *Geological Society of America Bulletin* was 'pretty convincing' and asking why I had not shown him all those detailed photographs when he had visited. It was true that I had not shown all my material to Anderson or his friend Goldring when the latter visited our department, because I suspected Anderson had his eye more on my material than my thesis. The hurriedly drafted paper dispatched to the journal by Anderson, listing me as second author, proved that my suspicions had been well founded. Fortunately for me, the department was expanding and the new faculty members were not pro-Anderson.

In the fall of 1968, Dr E.R.W. Neale, then heading the Appalachian Geology section in the Geological Survey of Canada, joined as professor and head of the geology department at Memorial University. Dr Neale remained in this position till after I had left Memorial in 1969. He moved to Calgary in western Canada in 1976.

A second addition to the faculty was Dr Hank Williams, a native of St John's, who was the first graduate of the geology department of Memorial University, a recipient of the Governor General's Gold Medal, and had also come from the Appalachian Geology Section of the Geological Survey of Canada. Another addition was Arthur F. King, who also belonged to Newfoundland and had done research in England. He specialized in sedimentology and joined the department in the academic year 1967-8.

Soon after he joined the department, Professor Neale invited each research student for a chat, to check on the status of our theses and other research work. That finally gave me an opportunity to report what Anderson had done. I still remember how I sat at the centre of the large room, with teachers all around, and narrated the story of my odyssey from India to St John's and, finally, of how my supervisor had misappropriated all my work.

The following morning, Professor Williams said: 'Your point was well taken.' Thereafter, Professor Neale constituted a supervisory committee for me, comprising Dr Hank Williams, Dr A.F. King, and M.M. Anderson, whom I could approach for any difficulty. I began showing my thesis, chapter by chapter, to Dr Williams who painstakingly edited it and offered me encouragement. It was thanks to him that the thesis was finally submitted later that year. Before its submission the faculty members of the department also visited my area in a group and I explained the work I had done and showed them the rest of the fossils. They were all convinced by my interpretation of the rocks and fossils. I have mentioned this visit in my thesis.

Recently, Prof Hank Williams sent me a photograph taken by him during that visit. I am still grateful to him for all his help. Had he not edited my thesis and meticulously corrected my language, I feel certain I would never would have got my degree the following year.

Meanwhile, I had presented my work before the faculty and students, and it was thoroughly debated. I remember Dr A.F. King asked during this seminar: 'What was the food of the animals you are talking about'? I said: 'I do not think there was anything like food at that time'. Everyone had laughed, but the question remains unanswered.

Although I was able to make many contributions to the mapping of that remote Mistaken Point area, it was primarily for the discovery of the fossils that I was awarded my degree. That was the first and perhaps the only undisputed fossil assemblage in the whole of North America at the time.

My research paper of 1969 was universally acclaimed in the geo-scientific community. Even the editor of the *Geological Society of America Bulletin* had written to me that I could get a larger audience in journals like *Science* or *American Scientist* but selfishly, however, I would like you to let us have it. With these remarks the editor accepted the paper for publication. This, I thought, was the greatest honour a young geologist could receive.

As letters poured in from scientists around the world, I began realizing the enormity of what I had found. The fossils bore similarities to others found earlier in Leicestershire in England, suggesting that Europe and Canada were at one point possibly one single land mass. Also, not only were they the remains of a previously unknown species, but were changing everything people had believed about the Precambrian era. Until I spotted those patterns in the rock, there had only been evidence of single-celled organisms, like bacteria and algae, in the Precambrian rocks of north America. My discovery has taken the story of life much deeper in time, now almost to the beginning of Metazoa (multi-celled animals) in the time span.

Earlier, not many were ready to accept the Darwinian theory that all life forms are related and have descended from a common ancestor. This disbelief was not without reason. There was an absence of fossil record of rocks older than the Cambrian era to support the theory of evolution of life on earth. Martin Glaessner in Australia was making an all out effort to prove that present day life evolved from the Ediacaran forms and has discussed my fossils in his book *Dawn of Animal Life* published in the US in1984. I was the first geologist to identify the Mistaken Point fossils as those of soft- bodied animals classified as Phylum Coelenterata (an animal group), based on such a well-documented record. After many twists and turns the geo-scientific community now tends to take the same position.

At that time my fossils were providing a link between those relatively primitive Precambrian forms of life and the fauna that inhabited the earth subsequently. They were changing the understanding of the evolution of life on earth, and helping identify the missing link in Darwin's Theory of Evolution.

'what is to be done?'

Sometimes, you *arrive* at a crossroad, sometimes you have to *create* one. I was a discoverer, I had postgraduate degrees from India and Canada. There were scholarships for further studies from across the continent but for some reason my life felt empty. The yellow lamps in my room, which I had gazed at with such pride when I first arrived, now only reminded me more acutely of the thousands groping in the dark. Why should I have had the opportunities I had, when so many others had yearned for them as acutely; tried as hard? Every so often, like a recurring dream, I would hear our voices as we shouted and laughed on that long, long walk to school. I would see the many classmates who had had to drop out, defeat written all over their faces, before they had even embarked on their lives. I had sworn to never forget; knew I had to return.

In the academic year 1967–8, the Indian community at St John's formed an organization called the Friends of India Association. I was elected its first general secretary. This could be a beginning, I remember thinking. Instead, it was all fun and games. We organized cultural programmes and celebrated the principal Indian festivals together. Foreigners interested in India would attend the meetings in traditional Indian attire, as we did ourselves, laughing at one another's dhotis and kurtas. We organized seminars too, complete with serious-sounding names and endless discussions on the many tragic problems facing our nation and the many solutions that 'could just work'. It was all talk and I wasn't sad to move on.

I was awarded a master's degree in May 1969 and had to move to another university for the PhD (the department of geology at Memorial University did not have a doctoral programme). While I was consumed by a churning of thoughts and was confronting a dilemma, I had offers of scholarships from several universities across north America. Professor Neale, the head of department, advised me to pick a small place, and suggested I take Carleton in Ottawa, the Canadian capital. I accepted his advice.

That very year, soon after I left for Ottawa, a press release was issued from St John's and printed in the newspaper *Globe and Mail,* published from Toronto. This time, my work was credited to 'S.B. Misra, now at Carleton University, Ottawa, and Paul Thompson of St John's'.

The headline read: 'A missing link?' The release went on to describe how 'an Indian graduate student and his assistant ... Paul Thompson of St John's' had found the famed fossils. It also went on to quote Professor M.M. Anderson, 'who was continuing the work at Memorial' as saying that the fossils indicate that complex organisms existed much earlier in geological history than was once thought, and he hoped to find further evidence of this. I was aghast. Paul Thompson had helped chip away at stone and carried it to my car! When would such absurdities end?

To be fair to Paul Thompson, he never laid claim to any part of the discovery. Anderson had, meanwhile, repeated the statement that the fossils were discovered by 'S.B. Misra and Paul Thompson' in a research paper in 1978, nine years later.

He never made a claim for himself, but he created sufficient confusion so that Gehling and Narbonne in their research paper of

2007 mentioned that 'one species of the spindle-shaped organisms' was discovered by M.M. Anderson, and Narbonne had earlier written on his web page that the fossils were discovered by 'faculty and students' of Memorial University.

I decided to leave them to their silliness and focus on the PhD. I was happy at Carleton. It had a much bigger campus than Memorial, and had a much larger Indian community. I even had a friend there, Nirankar Prasad from ONGC days. Prasad, a few years my senior in Canada, had a master's degree too and was now working with the Geological Survey of Canada.

When I got to Carleton in September, I also realized I had an (albeit tiny) fan base! People actually knew my name. A few days after completing my admission formalities, I was at the Bank of Nova Scotia on campus to open my account when a student standing beside me read my name on my forms and asked: 'Are you the same Misra who discovered the fossils?' I politely replied that I was, quietly beaming within.

Decades later, in 2009, I received a letter from a IX-th grade Canadian student Bridget Cameron, which made my day:

> Dear Dr Misra,
>
> I am a grade 9 student at Mobile Central High, in Witless Bay Newfoundland. For our Social Studies class we have been asked to present a biography of someone who has discovered a piece of heritage here in Newfoundland. I choose to write my report on you, because you discovered the fossils at Mistaken Point. I was wondering if you could give me some information on yourself and how you discovered the fossils, and what you are currently working on today. Thanks so much,
>
> Bridget Cameron

The geology department of Carleton University was headed by Professor Raymond W. Yole, who had offered me a Demonstrating (Teaching) Stipend of 1280 Canadian dollars per term. This was in addition to the research scholarship of 250 Canadian dollars per month which was to be given to me from the research grant of Dr J.A. Donaldson, with whom I was to work on my PhD thesis. I was comfortable with the financial assistance and the academic atmosphere in the department and the campus.

It was at around this time that I almost became addicted to coffee! Like an alcoholic, I remember thinking with horror. Every day at 11 a.m. I would feel the irresistible urge, no matter where I was, be it even in the laboratory or library, to go to the cafeteria for a cup of coffee before I could resume my work. I felt terrible; quite degenerate. I would never know whether it was due to the restlessness within me but I knew I must overcome it.

'This is becoming quite a difficulty, Misra,' I reprimanded myself, 'you have to take the matter in hand ... once and for all.' I decided to go cold turkey, and stopped drinking coffee altogether. It was now harder to stay up at night, but I felt it was worth it.

I was now writing my second paper on the Mistaken Point fossils, later accepted for publication by the *Geological Society of America Bulletin* and published in 1971. Professor Donaldson, who edited the manuscript of my paper, was an environmentalist and was deeply involved in research in the Northwestern Territories in Canada, where I would have gone to do my mapping had I continued.

By the time I had completed my paper, the holiday season had come around. For Christmas, all the students in the hostel were invited to one home or another in the town for a traditional dinner. I often wondered how they decided who would hold these traditional dinners. Obviously everyone couldn't, or there'd be no one to cook for! Besides, who would volunteer for all that trouble and expense? Don't worry your head about it, I told myself, it's obviously one of those cultural things that you can only understand from the inside.

My Christmas dinner, now that I was eating some non-vegetarian food, was delicious, and the family hosting it was deeply interested in India and wanted to know all about our country and its culture and history. I enjoyed the evening thoroughly and remembered with considerable sadness how my Russian friend V.V. Denisov at ONGC had tried to give me such a wonderful farewell with a similarly elaborate meal at Ankleswar.

There was a large library at Carleton, where I browsed through books on many subjects. Once, I encountered a book called *Voyage to America*, describing how the social reformer Swami Vivekananda had participated in the Parliament of World Religions in Chicago on 11 September 1893! I read it from beginning to end and felt proud of my country. There was another book, *Netaji at the Crossroads*, which was equally inspiring. It surprises me that, even today, such books are not readily available where they should be: in India.

I made many new Indian friends through Nirankar Prasad in Ottawa. They were from all over: Punjab, Haryana, Uttar Pradesh, Bihar, and Kerala. Most of them were doing PhDs, some were studying engineering. They were all keen to help their country, and this time the agenda included more than fireworks on Diwali and sitting around in kurtas, talking. One of my new friends, V.V.N. Simharao, worked at Microsystems International, a subsidiary of Bell Canada, and had rented a penthouse with a large sitting room on the fourteenth floor at 73, Woodridge Crescent. The club had a swimming pool, tennis court, and indoor sports facilities and soon became a favourite hangout for the rest of us, especially on weekends.

As we talked about India and what we wanted to do if we returned home, Simha would take notes and file them away. One day, Simha pasted a large, white sticker on the file and wrote: '*Kya kiya jaye*? (What is to be done?)'

After that, somehow, our discussions became more serious. We analysed what was ailing our nation's economy, and what we could do to help. Kamal from Punjab suggested that we support India while remaining in Canada. Simha suggested we pick a place and start employment-generating projects such as poultry-raising, dairying, and fish farms, but he was not sure where he wanted to do these things.I had my plan, and my location. I wanted to start a school in Deora.

'Misra was the only person who seemed absolutely certain of what he wanted to do,' Simha wrote in his minutes. 'He was less vocal most of the time, but when asked about his plan, he declared without hesitation that he wanted to start a secondary school in his native village as it did not have one at the time. He also determined to quit his PhD research and return to India.'

I remember that meeting so well. I remember thinking to myself: 'I'm actually going to do this. I'm going back, but I'm going to change Deora.' Simha was curious and asked, 'Why your native village'. I told him it was a really backward area. He said there were many backward areas and we could probably choose a more deserving one. I remember answering: 'If you visit my village and think there is any place more backward, we will shift our project.' Simha did visit Deora in July 1972. 'You were right,' he said.

Of the ten people in the group, thirty-year-old Simharao of East Godavari district in Andhra Pradesh understood how I felt better than any of the others. His village at least had a primary school, but from Class 6 to Class 12, he had travelled 15 kilometres by bullock cart. He too had grown up with shoes that could only be worn on special occasions, and had to leave home at age eleven to live with his grandmother so he wouldn't drown wading across a torrid rivulet to school in the monsoon. His father, Venkat Rao, had maintained land records for a living, till he quit and returned to his village to oversee work on his large land holdings. They were not badly off, Simha's family; theirs was just the average life of the rural Indian.

When Simha moved to a nearby town for Class 12, his two brothers and cousins followed him. His father moved too, to take care of them. There was no electricity even in the town, so the boys would cluster like moths around the only lantern, while Simha's father supervised their studies.

After Simha and his brothers enrolled at Andhra University, his father sold his fields one by one to pay their fees. Simharao did a master's in Physics; his brothers studied Mechanical Engineering and Economics respectively. His father now lived with him, talking proudly of his sons to anyone who would listen. Simha had truly come a long way, from that dark hut to a penthouse with a Mustang parked way below. For me, his penthouse was the crossroad I would create. Once I had said it out loud, it was as if I could wait no longer.

The idea of a life of riches and fame, the luxury of the physical comforts we were surrounded by, the prospect of earning big bucks and buying a string of status symbols to decorate our lives in North America all seemed so hollow.

I became depressed and withdrawn. Some of my friends noticed and tried to cheer me up. Simha took me to lovely Getnau Park for a picnic with his family. A few days later, Nirankar took me to the Niagara Falls, driving all the way from Ottawa. I had already seen Niagara from the Canadian side, and I sulked.

I think Simha sensed it was the end of the joyride for me. He stopped the picturesque picnics and tourist spots, and began taking me to agricultural farms to show me how grain was stored in silos and how cows could be fed and milked mechanically. I saw a mechanized poultry farm of 5,000 birds, managed perhaps by two or three people. It was as if he knew I was on my way home, and he wanted to ensure I took it all in before I set off.

It was at around this time that Beena, my college friend Ravi Shanker's younger sister, got married and moved to the US with her husband, Dr Kedar Verma of Bilaspur in Madhya Pradesh. They visited Ottawa in early 1970, and we stayed together at Nirankar's place for two or three days. They too seemed to sense my restlessness and I remember Kedar asking what was wrong. In a flood, I told him of our meetings in the penthouse and my dream school. 'But why now,' he asked. There will always be another exam, a new project, I said, more to myself than him. If I don't do it now, I fear I never will. I fear I will let down all the people who helped me through those years. My father, Zalim Singh, the quiet primary teacher who walked to school and was never late, Munshi Sharda Baksh Singh, who taught students after hours for free and smoked alone in a little mud room at the back. Kedar seemed to understand, and shocked me by offering his huge plot of land in Madhya Pradesh for my project. He had, however, to stay on in the US and I did not know his area or his family, so I declined with thanks.

Moping around and generally depressed, it was at this time that I had my first, and only! drink in Canada. All my friends knew that I was a teetotaller, but at one of the campus parties, they insisted I try a little, and I agreed. I didn't know they were topping up my whiskey with rum through the night and soon I was pretty drunk. I decided to leave the party and headed back. I remember the distance seemed much longer, probably because I was weaving around in a zig-zag fashion, stopping every once in a while to give myself a very firm talking-to. Getting the key into the lock seemed to take an age. As I stumbled in, so did a few friends who had followed me back. How nice, I thought, they were worried. On the contrary, they began asking me all sorts of complicated questions about religion, politics, etcetera. I even recited the Hanuman Chalisa and verses from the Ramayan on request. Then they asked me what I thought of Ogilvy, our provost in the hostel. 'That son of a ...' Luckily, I had not completed the sentence when I noticed the tape-recorder. I stopped and ordered them out, furious as only a drunk man can be! I stayed off alcohol for the rest of my stay in Canada.

The academic session at Carleton University ended with the exams in April 1970. I had cleared most of the tests, but an oral discussion with a panel from the department had not gone well. The truth is, my heart wasn't even in my studies any longer. I had several options. Professor Donaldson had put up a notice on the board inviting applications for summer jobs in the Northwestern Territories. I could ask for one, or I could go back to Professor Brueckner, who had returned from his sabbatical, and work in Newfoundland. Alternatively, I could return home. The crossroad I had created lay before me. I talked it over with Simharao. He agreed that it was time to switch paths, and came to see me off at the airport. On 10 August 1970, I boarded a Syrian Airlines flight, that had the cheapest tickets, and returned to India via Damascus, Dubai, and Karachi.

I have always had mixed luck with flights, and this time was no different. The stopovers at Damascus and Dubai were nice and friendly, but Karachi was awful. All the passengers were allowed to go to the lounge of the airport for refreshments and some rest, except the Indians. We were not even allowed off the plane! Five years after the war, there was still a great deal of tension between the two countries. My plane landed in New Delhi on the afternoon of 11 August 1970: four days before Independence Day, I was home.

starting trouble

I didn't realize how much I had missed speaking in my mother tongue, Hindi, till I heard it again. I was back home amongst my own people. I had missed so many things. Our prime minister had changed: Lal Bahadur Shastriji had been succeeded by the strong-willed Indira Gandhi, daughter of the beloved Pandit Jawaharlal Nehru. The lady who had defeated the old guard and was trying to come to terms with the problems of India such as poverty and hunger. There was something they called Green Revolution taking root in Punjab (not many thought it would succeed, and there were numerous jokes about its optimistic name). Not least! the Hindi movies were all starting to feature a young man from Allahabad who the ladies just couldn't seem to get enough of: a young man called Amitabh Bachchan.

At New Delhi Railway Station, however, the sights and sounds were still the same: that welcoming, familiar assault on the senses. Everywhere, people were shouting, chasing trains, losing luggage.

Vendors were crying: '*Paan, bidi,* cigarette ... *chai, chai garam chai*'. There were so many people. I had forgotten what it was like to be part of one of the fastest growing populations on the planet. There were more people at the Delhi station, it seemed to me, than in all of Ottawa!

Even though I was severely jetlagged, and this time I knew what it was, it took just seconds for the old habits to kick back in. I elbowed my way to the ticket counter and got a reservation on the Lucknow Mail. By morning, I would be back in the city where it had all begun.

Getting off the train, my black attaché case in hand, the magnitude of what I had done, and what I was hoping to do next, began to sink in. I had a long way to go, and I wasn't sure where to start. For one thing, no one even knew I was back.

Outside Lucknow railway station, all on my own once again, I climbed into a cycle rickshaw and directed the driver to a hotel in Lalbagh with which I was familiar from my college days. On the way there, the rickshaw passed Kanya Kubja Degree College (now Jai Narain college), from where I had left for Canada. The streets, the people, the crowds ... they all looked the same, and I remember thinking to myself that things changed very slowly in my country.

I didn't get much sleep that night. I think I was in shock. I had wrenched myself out of my familiar groove in Canada, away from the profession I knew and excelled in, and now what? All night, as I lay in that cheap hotel room, I thought: Shiva Balak, you have come home to rescue Deora, but where are you going to begin?

In the rush of emotion, I had not done my homework properly. I had no land, relatively little money, and my expertise in identifying rocks wasn't exactly going to help me in that. I was really in no position to start work on providing education to the rural poor. I had spoken to no one about the project; had no plan ....

By the next morning, though, the terror had abated somewhat and I decided to take it one day at a time, at least for now. On 12 August 1970, I opened an account in Oriental Bank of Commerce in Hazaratganj, using my passport as proof of my identity.

After that, I decided to visit P.L. Bali, a kindly gentleman whose children I had tutored before I left for Canada. Bali was a migrant from

West Pakistan and had fled to India after Partition. We had grown very close, like family, in my final months as an assistant teacher at Jubilee Inter-College. I will never forget how overjoyed he had been when I told him of my Newfoundland scholarship.

I entered the door that was still so familiar to me. The family was sitting in the drawing room. The children, quite grown up now, looked at me for a while and there was an odd silence. Then one of the girls said: 'Master Sahib *to nahin hain* ? (Isn't he our teacher?)'. I said, '*Haan, pahchan to liya* (Yes, you have recognized me).'

Oh, the flutter that ensued. As tea was offered and biscuits and fried snacks had by all, I felt, for the first time since I had returned, that I was well and truly home. P.L. Bali's wife, Pushpa Bali, asked me where my luggage was. When I told her it was at the hotel, she looked at me in mock horror. Oh, how I had missed the warmth of my people. 'A hotel?' she shrieked. 'You must stay here, with us. Do you have no friends in Lucknow that you should stay in a hotel like a stranger?' Duly chastized, I brought my luggage over and stayed with the Balis for the following week.

Over the next few days, I broke it to Bali that this wasn't just a visit. I was not returning to Canada, I told him. I intended to work in my village, open a school. Bali was dismayed, but he was ready to listen. To generate money to run the school, I told him, I planned to start a poultry and dairy farm. Bali had some experience in farming: he still had a buffalo, and he had some chickens too. He kindly offered me a shed for a pilot project in poultry farming.

A little less disoriented after my talk with him, I decided to go to my village and do some groundwork there. I had just bought a ticket for Itaunja at Qaiserbagh bus stand when a young man came up to me and politely asked: '*Aap* Shiva Balak Daddu [one of my nicknames in the village] *hain* (Are you Brother Shiva Balak)?' I replied in the affirmative. He touched my feet in the traditional greeting of respect and took my luggage.

This young chap, Chaman Lal, was the grandson of Gulab Chaudhari, the head of the cobbler community in my village. He had completed high school from Bakshi-ka-Talab, a large village near Deora, and was now studying for the Basic Training Certificate, then the minimum qualification for primary school teachers. This was quite an achievement for a Scheduled Caste boy in those days and I was proud and impressed. Perhaps things were already changing in Deora, I remember thinking. Perhaps I had set an example before them to struggle and achieve, I wishfully thought.

Chaman Lal and I boarded the bus to Itaunja together and were there in an hour. Then I was back on the 12-kilometre road that had haunted me through senior primary school, walking the very distance that I had returned to shorten for others. On the way, I wondered what changes had come about in my village. Would there be other smart young men like Chaman Lal, bringing new light to their homes as they built better lives in the big world outside?

After walking for two hours and passing through the familiar villages of Mahona, Atasua, and Shahpur, the evening saw us back in Deora. Chaman Lal walked with me to my house and then rushed off to his own home in Chamarahi (the cobblers' area) to tell them of my return.

In the dying light, the village gathered to meet the young man who had flown across the seas to the land of white men, to study and live among them, and had now returned so suddenly without a word in advance. Some of them stared as if they had never seen me before, and I remember feeling a little unnerved, and also disappointed.

Nothing had changed in Deora; at least not for the better. My mud house was dilapidated and my family looked worse off than when I had left. I had been sending money to my father regularly, but I was now told that the crops had failed for the last few years, as each successive monsoon failed to arrive, and the money had been barely sufficient to keep the family going.

My father had also spent a large sum on a concrete well in our fields, one I had insisted he build so he could irrigate the land when the rains failed. The well proved to be a complete failure. Borewells and pumps were, however, rare in those days, so it had been our only chance.

It was the monsoon now in August 1970, and most of the houses in the village were crumbling in the rains. Inside, grain was still stored in huge mud vessels and edibles like lentils, flour, and condiments in earthen vessels stacked one over the other. The homes continued to be lit by earthen lamps and there was still only one brick house: that of Ganga Prasad, the moneylender.

I sat down on a *charpai* in the front room and people streamed in and took their seats on the other *charpais*, on the ground, and on the threshold. I rose every so often to touch the feet of my elders in greeting. Many of them touched my feet too, in respect. I was healthier and fairer, they all said. The young children, who had never seen me before, listened as the older ones explained where I had been. Then they wanted to touch me; feel my clothes. Many of the women whispered that I spoke differently, 'like a *gora*' (white man).

As their timidity wore off, the elders began asking me questions about the people in Canada, their life and their wealth. This is something I have never quite understood: our capacity to marvel at the riches of others and feel no resentment, and no urge to create some wealth of our own. We can never hear enough about movie stars, foreigners, even corrupt politicians, and how well they live. It's as if, because they have it, they deserve it, and because we don't, it follows that we don't deserve it either. In the end, and I see this still, as we move further from the cities, the people there are grateful just for the vicarious pleasure of peeping in at the window and experiencing it all at second-hand.

In the failing light in my father's crumbling house in Deora, I told the villagers of my plan to stay back and build a school. A stunned silence followed my announcement. Their expressions froze in confusion. Most were dismayed, while others seemed to think I was joking, or had perhaps lost my mind. My father made no suggestions or comments. He just seemed happy I was back.

Then some of the villagers began to talk about a school. 'Make it like Bakshi-ka-Talab,' said Suraj Lal Bajpai. Bakshi-ka-Talab, about 20 kilometre away, had a high school, built by a local politician Shyam Manohar Mishra after he became a legislator and trusted follower of C.B. Gupta, the then chief minister of Uttar Pradesh. Indeed, in those days, starting a school was often a stepping-stone to politics, just as the legal profession had been in the 1950s and '60s.

At my father's house, however, very few approved of my plan. Most of the villagers left muttering under their breaths about wasted opportunity and foolish ideas. Over the next few days, I tried to prove that I was serious about this. I began talking to the young men in the village about how we could go about building the structure once I had bought some land.

When I showed no signs of regaining my senses and fleeing back to glittering Canada, some imaginative stories began doing the rounds. Worried friends would come over every few days with a new rumour. Some had it I had lost my mind and the doctors had advised me to rest in a village. I would go back once I was cured. This theory seemed to have many takers. Another story was that I had married a Canadian girl in a moment of foolishness and run back to Deora to escape her.

There was serious concern in the minds of people about the viability of the school project. Recently Jagat Narain, my old friend, narrated an interesting conversation he had with his village folks in those days. It went like this: *'Chalega nahin, jungle mein kaun padhega'* (it will not succeed; who will study in the jungle) said one Ram Prakash of Atesua. Jagat replied, 'I know him, he will not fail'. When Ram Prakash, a primary school teacher then, said, *'Amrica se paisa laye hain, phoonk rahe hain'* (he has brought money from America and is wasting it). The third rumour was that I had been unsuccessful in Canada and lost my scholarship, but would be getting another one soon, after which I would be off again.

***

As the weeks passed and I showed no signs of leaving, though the villagers gradually began to believe that I was serious, I began looking for a piece of land and I finally found about eight acres that I thought would be sufficient. The plot was perfect: peaceful and green, and even at a slight elevation which meant it would not get flooded during the monsoon.

It was not however in Deora but in Kunaura village right next door, where I had beamed with pride when my first teacher, Zalim Singh, entered my name into a worn register in his one-room school in the spare room of a mud hut.

After some tough negotiations with the owner, I purchased the land from a certain Ibrahim, and he signed the sale deed. I started planning my school, and this was when the villagers really stepped up. They could not help with syllabi or teachers, or even finances, but as work began, people from five villages around Deora began streaming in, offering to help in the only way they knew, through *shramdan* or working without recompense on the proposed school land with their bare hands. *Shramdan* (voluntary labour) had built many small roads and check dams in our villages, now it was helping to build my school.

Some farmers teamed up to build a path to the plot. Others dug a well so that the students would have sufficient drinking water. They walked miles to the site every morning, worked all day, and went quietly home after sunset, never expecting anything in return. '*Chhokra jo kar raha hai, theek kar raha hai* (What the boy is doing is right),' I would hear them say when talking among themselves.

In Lucknow, however, many of my well-wishers were still puzzled. 'Why are you throwing away such a brilliant career,' my former teacher, Professor R.C. Misra, once asked me. 'I'm still here. I can help you find a job.' I tried to explain that I was not interested in a job. He brushed the explanation aside and demanded that I help him translate a book from English into Hindi. He thought he was doing me a favour, and I didn't have the heart to say no, so I helped him and simultaneously kept working on my project.

A couple of months later, work was progressing at a decent pace and it was time for Phase Two of my plan. My savings were drying up, so, in January 1971, P.L. Bali helped me kick off my pilot project in poultry farming with the generous gift of a tin shed measuring about 400 square feet, fitted with light bulbs inside, a tap nearby, and some open land in which to allow the chicks to scratch about. A local poultry inspector helped me arrange the litter (ground up paddy husk) on the floor of the shed and set up water bowls for the birds, and then ordered me off to buy day-old chicks from the hatchery at Bakshi-ka-Talab.

I actually saw my chicks come into the world at the hatchery. It was a wonderful experience, watching them stamp their way out of their eggs in the incubators. I bought 300 chicks at one rupee per chick and the poultry department arranged to transport them to Lucknow for me.

The poultry unit required constant attention for the first few days, and I did all the work myself. As Simharao said in one of his letters, my entire journey had been so paradoxical: A Brahmin nicknamed Panditji dealing in poultry to enable him to earn enough to start a school. It's a miracle the entire village didn't write me off as a lunatic!

The principal problem in the poultry business was the feeding schedule, and keeping the chicks safe from cats. All the water bowls too had to be kept clean or the birds would get sick and die. Also, the chicks had to be vaccinated to prevent them from getting diseases like smallpox or cholera. Like a mother hen, I had to keep an eye out for any signs of illness, and sick birds had to be identified immediately and separated from the rest.

After about three months of this, it was finally time to make good on my investment. The male chicks were separated from the female ones for the final month, and then it was time to sell the former and pamper the latter. The hens were given special attention; open wooden boxes were kept in shady corners of the shed for them to lay their eggs.

The first egg was laid in the first week of June 1971, and I was thrilled. Had it had been anything else, I would have rushed with that first fruit of my labour to the temple, to offer it up in thanks. This was, however, an egg! And the Brahmin gods, I felt certain, would be quite sullen at such an inappropriate offering.

Well, production averaged about 70 per cent, which meant 70 eggs per 100 birds each day. This was a good average for the 'white leghorn' variety of hens that we had. The local varieties had a lower average. Marketing the eggs was no problem, so long as I had Bali as frontman. As a Brahmin, I did not think it would be a good idea to sell the eggs myself in a primitive village like Deora, so wholesalers would come to his house and buy at the rate of half a rupee per egg.

That same week in June, I also became the legal owner of my plot in Kunaura. The sale deed cost me Rs 10,500. The village headman Janki Prasad and Lachhman Bajpai, the village elder who had seen the ghosts near the well at the big orchard near Atesua and had not scolded me when I had slipped in a puddle and dissolved his three kilos of sugar, were witnesses to the deed.

I had another gift from providence at this time. Professor R.C. Misra, who had been trying ever since I returned to get me to follow a career in geology, asked me during one of my courtesy calls to help a private company in a short-term exploration programme for iron and manganese in Madhya Pradesh. The company, Ram Ji Gopal Ji Pvt Ltd, was offering Rs 1,500 a month, a great salary for 1971. I accepted the offer with some reluctance because I thought I was deviating from my goal. My project could however utilize some more capital.

I left my chickens in Bali's care and set off for Sidhi in Madhya Pradesh. There, I reported to Pandey, the regional director of the company, only to find that he and a certain Chandra Kishore Shukla alias Bacchu, some sort of chemist who was the only other employee at the 'regional headquarters', were living in a rented house with no laboratory and no office. I was going to have to start from scratch.

'are your degrees genuine?'

As the lone geologist prospecting for iron and manganese on behalf of Ram Ji Gopal Ji Pvt Ltd, I had to walk long distances, day after day, looking for tell-tale signs of these metals. I had a few local people to guide me and carry my luggage (hopefully, none of them would later lay claim to any discoveries I might make here, I playfully remember thinking to myself).

By and large, the guides were friendly and helpful, but science was not their strong point. One day I asked the labourers, who belonged to the Kole tribe, the distance to a particular village. They said it was three miles. That shouldn't take long, I smiled. There were no smiles in response. Well, I eventually found out why. We had been walking about two hours when I finally asked why we weren't there yet. Two more miles, the man said, looking surprised at my impatience. I knew I had already walked at least five miles. Exasperated, I asked: 'How do you measure your miles?'

'We put a big leaf on our head,' said the man, demonstrating this absurd technique with his long arms as he spoke. 'Then we sprinkle some water on it. When the leaf has dried, the distance covered is one mile.' I gaped at him in incredulity.

'What if it's cloudy ... or raining?' Then, we just walk till we get there, the man explained, frowning at me puzzled, as if I were the one missing the point. I ordered him to guide us back to Sidhi, leaves on heads or not. I would not be using them, or their unique system of measurement, again.

They had lots of strange customs, the tribes of Madhya Pradesh. I remember a friend of mine from nearby Rewa telling me how the Bhil tribes of western Madhya Pradesh would loot anyone they could lay their hands on, provided they could first defeat him in unarmed combat. In that way, they felt they had not taken his belongings without effort. Muslims in my area would call it '*halal*', or using positive effort. Likewise, if a boy from this tribe wished to marry a particular girl, he had to first carry her on his shoulders for a set distance, running from point to point in front of an audience of the entire community, to prove he was good enough for her. The larger women must be happy, I remember thinking, believing that they had matchmakers and arranged marriages as backup.

Well, after surveying the area for a couple of months on behalf of Ram Ji Gopal Ji Pvt Ltd, I submitted my report to the regional director Pandey: the quantity (reserve) of iron on their leased area was too small, and the percentage of manganese too low. It would not be possible to build the ferromanganese plant here, as they had envisaged. I had, however, seen signs of significant amounts of copper on their land. Unfortunately, they did not have the permission to explore for this metal. My job done, I returned to Deora and the task of completing my school.

In one corner of my plot, my fellow villagers and I began work on a little brick structure measuring 40 ft by 10 ft, with two doors facing east (for good luck). The room was ready by January 1972. Thatching was fixed on the eastern and western walls, creating a shaded area of about 1,200 sq. ft. That was all I could afford, and I thought it was a decent start.

It was now, as I set out on my loneliest endeavour so far, that I began to feel for the first time that it would be nice to have the companionship and support of a wife. I was, however, also clear about the kind of wife I wanted. She had to be educated, and had to care as much as I did about educating the rural poor. The draw of a 'foreign-returned boy' was so strong that I was still getting plenty of proposals, notwithstanding my unemployed status and even the rumours of my weakened state of mind! Most of the proposals came with decent offers of dowry, but nearly all the women were high-school dropouts. One proposal came with Rs 40,000 and other property as dowry, a remarkable offer at the time, but the girl was only a matriculate.

Then there was also the recurring proposal, from Chandra Kishore (Bacchu), the chemist I had worked with at Ram Ji Gopal Ji. He insisted his cousin would be perfect for me, but the girl was a Lucknow brat. She had grown up in the big city. I tried to politely explain that it seemed to me like a match made in hell. However, Bacchu would not give up. He passed on the address of my village to the girl's father, Krishna Lal Shukla, in Lucknow, so that he could make enquiries about me and my family.

Shuklaji, a hefty gentleman, did not want to rely on local gossip for his information. Therefore, though unaccustomed to travelling long distances, he called on a rail-thin friend Ram Autar Verma to help him get to Itaunja, where he heard I had gone to school. There, he settled down at a tea stall I had been known to frequent, sipped on some sugary sweet tea, and began to ask the stall owner, who had some relatives in Deora and knew me well, about me.

There was something peculiar about the tea. Misra, the shop-owner, used to put a pinch of salt in it and that was his brand.

The shop-owner, like all chaiwallahs, loved to talk. Soon, he told Shuklaji my entire story: school, college, Canada, and back ... the works. Shuklaji apparently liked what he heard; liked it enough to set off immediately for Deora to meet me himself. The rail-thin Verma was ordered off to hire a cycle and Shuklaji was installed on the carrier. That cycle was a sight to behold, I believe, rearing on its back wheels like an agitated horse as the rail-thin friend tried to pedal them forward. It was only with great effort and perseverance that the duo reached Deora. Then, after all this trouble, I wasn't even there. Both men were sorely disappointed. I thought it was quite a pity, but I was still very certain that I didn't want to marry the Lucknow brat. It was therefore probably a good thing, I remember thinking to myself, that it had ended before it began.

Shuklaji was however nothing but thorough, and his wife Tara Devi was persistent. She dropped in at the Bali home a few days later and met me. Then she went home and persuaded her husband to renew his efforts to finalize a match. She had a kind of premonition, she told me in later years; a feeling that I was meant for her daughter. She told me once that I had appeared in her dreams and had spoken pleasantly to her. She was also concerned, she laughingly admitted, that her daughter Nirmala was twenty-five and quite aged by Brahmin standards.

By the time Shuklaji finally met me in Lucknow, I had become quite a pro at turning people away. 'If you think I'm a good match because I'm back from Canada and have a great job with a good salary,' I told him, 'I have to tell you I have left it all behind and do not intend to work as a geologist again.' Shuklaji brushed aside my carefully prepared speech: 'Are your degrees genuine?' he asked. 'Yes,' I said, a little startled. 'They are genuine.' Apparently, that was all he wanted to know. He nodded to me politely and left a few minutes later. Now the Balis were in the game too. 'If you do not wish to meet Nirmala formally,' said Bali's wife, Pushpa Devi, 'I will think of a way to meet her first. Then I will come back and tell you all about her.'

Pushpa Devi thereupon set off for Jauhari Inter College, where Nirmala was the principal, and met her on the pretext of buying an admission form. All was going well, till Nirmala asked for the name of the intended student. Poor well-meaning Pushpa Devi fumbled and fled. She hadn't really thought her plan through … but she had to meet Nirmala. [My wife later told me she never even paid for the form!]

The next day, the Balis and I dropped by Nirmala's office. We chatted in a rather relaxed way, posing as acquaintances of her father, though I suspect she realized who I was when the Balis introduced me as 'Misraji'.

Well, I had seen Nirmala, and I had to admit, her mother was right: there was something about her. She was beautiful, and confident, and so very smart. She was already principal of the little college, but would she be able to adjust to village life?

The Shuklas were the complete opposite of my family. They were rich landlords, with acres of land in Comilla (now in Bangladesh) and Sumerpur in district Unnao in Uttar Pradesh. They were all well educated. Shuklaji was a graduate, his brother Krishna Kishore had a law degree, and his cousins, Brij Kishore and Shyam Lal, were also graduates.

Most of their education had been in Comilla and they spoke fluent Bengali. The four brothers had twenty-three children between them, ten girls and thirteen boys. They all managed their own land, except for Shuklaji, who had defied the family norms and accepted a job. Such 'service' was generally looked down upon by the Shuklas, even though he was working at the state secretariat in Lucknow.

Nirmala was the eldest of seven children born to Shuklaji and Tara Devi. Their first child, a girl, had died soon after birth. Nirmala had a sister and four brothers. That was pretty much all I knew about her, but once I had shown interest, Pushpa Bali took it from there. She met Tara Devi on several occasions and tested Nirmala's skills in knitting, cooking, and singing!

I, much like her father, had only one concern: Were her degrees genuine? Nirmala got terribly angry when I first called for her certificates. She would not marry a person, she said, who did not trust her qualifications. Eventually her mother prevailed upon her and Nirmala agreed to send her degrees. We got to talking, largely through relatives, of course, and Nirmala said she had no objection to moving to a village and helping me set up my school. She now says she never actually thought a 'Canada-returned' boy would actually sentence himself to life in a village. Well, I didn't know whether she was hoping I would eventually leave, and she didn't know I was planning to stay but as it happened, as Simha so aptly put it, our two souls were soon betrothed to one another in marriage. 'At some point in time, it would appear that the girl, Nirmala Shukla, agreed to be married, ' Simha wrote in his diary. 'It was a marvellous journey on which this pair embarked: she commanding by nature but never demanding, he a man of concept, driven by analysis, sometimes by intuition of the right order.'

'Diversity was obvious,' Simha went on to say, 'but both went along as a team, not by compromise, but probably because both possessed a nature to take a milder position when the other was dominant.'

It may sound like the perfect marriage now, but the initial days were tough for my wife. I think the culture shock began the night of the pre-wedding feast at the groom's house. There were so many mosquitoes in our village, and no fans or lights, because there was still no electricity, that Bacchu joked the following morning that if the bedbugs in his cot had not held him back, the mosquitoes would surely have spirited him away. Bacchu wasn't exaggerating: that's what village life was like.

We agreed to keep our wedding as simple as we could without upsetting either of our families. There was no question of dowry and I wanted as little of the usual quibbling over costs and expenses as possible. Other than the fact that I completed the traditional parade to the bride's house earlier than anyone had expected, and was perhaps the only groom ever to arrive on time in the history of our ancient culture, all went smoothly. On the evening of 14 May 1972, Nirmala and I were married.

Looking back now, I think it was probably the next morning, as she loaded her bags on to a taxi bound for Itaunja, that the realization of all she was leaving behind began to set in. A decorated palanquin awaited my bride at Itaunja, meant to carry her in great state to her new home in Deora. A few relatives and I were to chug home in a truck as the palanquin moved alongside. We soon abandoned this grand plan. It was too hot and the going too slow, so we loaded the palanquin on to the truck and set off, Nirmala and I in full wedding regalia glittering on the front seat.

On the outskirts of the village, the palanquin was unloaded and the bride reinstalled. I didn't see it then, but we were already working together as a team, and the no-nonsense balance between common sense and tradition that we found that first day would be the hallmark of our marriage, getting us through some fairly rough times. These rough times began soon enough. My lovely, young wife, the descendant of generations of wealthy *zamindars,* who had spent her youth fashioning her hair after the latest Hindi film heroines and had travelled alone by train to her college in the next district was now sleeping on a charpai in a suffocating *kothari* (room) with no indoor plumbing. Small mud pellets dropped from the ceiling as mosquitoes sang in her ears.

I was detained outside the house by elders on the grounds that the *muhurat* for the *chatursi* (groom's entry into the house) was not auspicious. I waited for a few hours and finally defied the custom. At least we were together in the mud house.

The next morning, when it was still dark, the women took a *lota* (metallic vessel) full of water each and asked Nirmala to come with them to the orchards. There, they sat down and relieved themselves, motioning to Nirmala to sit too. My bewildered bride just stared at them and remained standing: even in her ancestral village of Sumerpur there had been latrines in their house.

For days, Nirmala would not use the orchard 'toilet'. Eventually, however, the shock wore off and she joined the group. I can't imagine how hard it must have been for her, but she never uttered a word of complaint.

A few weeks after our wedding, I told Nirmala I would like to take her to Khajuraho. She was thrilled, imagining it would be some kind of honeymoon. Seeing her face light up, I didn't have the heart to tell her my real destination was Sidhi. I needed to withdraw money I had deposited in the local bank when I was working there.

Our first stop after Lucknow was Allahabad, where we stopped to take a dip at Sangam, the confluence of the three holy rivers: the mighty Ganga, the famed Yamuna, and the invisible Saraswati.

We were taken to the sacred spot by a boatman and a Hindu priest. At the Sangam, the priest told me to tie Nirmala's sari to my kurta, and then, just as we were bowing our heads to pray, he began haggling over his fee. We unfolded our hands and thrashed it out till we had arrived at a mutually acceptable figure: I would later learn this is a precursor to most rituals for pilgrims at holy spots in India.

Finally, he chanted the prayers and ordered us to drop the coconut and flower offerings he had brought into the water, and give him his money. Then he pocketed his fee, leant over the other side of the boat and, to my utter dismay, swooped up our coconut as it floated past. I was miserable at the thought that our holy coconut had probably been used by some pilgrim before us ... and would be used again. Anyhow, our union had been blessed at one of the most sacred spots in the Hindu tradition and we would have to content ourselves with sharing the coconut.

We got to Sidhi and I closed my account and withdrew my money. On our return journey, I took my wife to Khajuraho as promised, but it was so hot that we could scarcely bear it. We were nonetheless determined to make the trip a memorable one and, in order to preserve it for posterity, I took numerous photographs of my wife from different angles in various corners of the carved temples.

We returned to Lucknow by bus, our little vacation over. Sadly, the reel proved to be a dud. When they developed the frames at the little photo studio in Lucknow, not a single picture emerged. The reel had not moved an inch: perhaps the gods of sculpture did not think it fit to see Nirmala in such an exotic setting.

Not long after our 'accidental honeymoon', as we like to call it now, in the last week of June I got some pamphlets printed and distributed in the area to announce the opening of my school at Kunaura. On 1 July 1972, we took the sofa and chairs we had received as gifts at our wedding and placed them in the make-believe office. It was the only furniture we had, but I remember thinking it looked quite impressive. We decided that for the classrooms, we would arrange jute matting after some admissions had taken place. The opening of the school was big news for miles around, but most of our early visitors seemed keener to have a look around than to send their children there to study. Some eventually decided to send their sons and brothers but the prospect of girls being sent to school seemed to amuse them no end.

It was a small cluster of families in a village called Ayodhyanagari, migrants from Bihar, who first realized the school's potential. They were the first to start sending their children, boys and girls alike, to our class. Soon, children from other villages were streaming in too. By the end of the month we had an impressive 100 students, and quite a staff crunch.

Nirmala and I were honorary teachers, but we had to appoint a third teacher to help handle the kids, and he needed to be paid a salary. This third teacher, Shripal was incidentally the son of Suraj Lal Bajpai, one of the men who had helped kidnap me from Misirpur in my childhood.

Parents of none of our students could afford to pay fees so, for all the expenses, I had to depend heavily on my savings from Canada as the poultry business had sort of fizzled out and the agricultural land on my plot had not yet begun yielding a crop.

Of my two stepbrothers, Gangadhar had come to my rescue and was looking after my agricultural land. He was preparing for his intermediate exams and would come to the school to share some of the teaching work. The younger one, Mishri Lal, was still studying: in our school!

V.V.N. Simharao, one of the ten concerned Indians from my Canada days, had returned to India at about this time and visited the school with his wife Bhanumati. In a recent meeting in Delhi he told me how he had taken one look at our village, with no roads, no power, no clean drinking water, and barren fields, and in a flash understood what I had meant in Canada when I had said that if he could find a more backward part of India, I would shift my project there. When he got to our school, he said, he was thrilled to see so many girls studying there; also to see scheduled caste children sitting side by side with upper-caste Hindus.

Once the monsoon set in, in July, the entire area was flooded and Shripal, Nirmala, and I had to wade through knee-deep water to get to our school from Deora. It was exhausting and dreadfully uncomfortable trying to work all day in our soaked clothes. I sometimes wondered whether this would be the breaking point for Nirmala. After all, how long could she be expected to put up with this?

Nirmala, however, in her typically level-headed way, chose to find a solution rather than complain. She carried a spare set of clothes every day, washed up and changed at the school, and cheerfully got down to work. She had also began reaching out to the villagers, listening to their problems, and talking to them about why it was important for them to send their children to school. Soon, she had carved out an identity for herself: no mean feat in a culture where women were never even referred to by name but rather in relation to the men in their lives. Nirmala herself was initially known as 'Canada *wali bhabhi* (sister-in-law from Canada)' or 'Misraji *ki bahu* (Misraji's daughter-in-law)'. Gradually however she acquired a different name: Principal Sahiba.

In Deora, Nirmala organized group-singing events in the evenings which became very popular with the women. She also got the boys and girls together to act in skits, helping develop their personality and confidence. A turning point, I think, was her Independence Day celebration in 1972. Just three months old in our village, she organized a microphone, a great treat for Deora, and gave a speech about girls and education and progress that drew great applause and was quoted for years as the last word in any arguments on those issues. The following morning, it was still all the buzz, and one villager gleefully told me: '*Bahuria ka bhashan aap se khoob acchha raha* (Daughter-in-law's lecture was better than yours).'

At around that time I came into contact with a Dalit youth, Badlu (now sixty-seven), of Deora. Badlu remembers it all. He says the Principal Sahiba had encouraged him to celebrate Ravidas Jayanti (a celebration eulogizing Sant Ravidas), and even sent artists from our school to their stage. This was the beginning of emancipation of the Scheduled Castes in my village. For me, the greatest achievement of that first term was a play we staged for the village in September 1972. Badlu, a scheduled caste boy, played King Dasharath, sitting proudly on a lofty throne covered in gold chart paper. A Brahmin, Om Prakash Tewari, played Shravan, the legendary son devoted to his impoverished, blind parents and Kanhaiya Lal, another Brahmin, played Shravan's blind father. Shravan Kumar is killed at the end of the play by the powerful Dashrath (Badlu) through an error of judgement. In a village where people from the Scheduled Castes had to rise to their feet if an upper-caste Hindu was passing, this was a historic moment for us. Banshi Bajpai of 'Maulvi Sahib *machhli pakad lai'* fame had commented 'a cobbler is seated on the throne'. I had ignored the comment. On a later occasion Badlu says he was crying because the rains had washed off the stage set up by them for Ravidas Jayanti. 'Principal Sahiba came,' he says, and said 'why are you crying? Get up and clean; everything will be all right by the evening'.

The weather cleared and they were able to stage a play that night.

Badlu says that Principal Sahiba used to arrange rehearsals of plays to be staged in the school as well as on the occasion of Ravidas Jayanti. Many scheduled-caste boys had learnt to stage a play, including Chaman Lal, Badlu, Basant, and others. Even today they celebrate Ravidas Jayanti without fear of Brahmins. Once the Brahmins of Deora had planned to disrupt their procession but Principal Sahiba had stopped them, says Badlu. Jagmohan Bajpai of Shahpur confirms that if we were not with these people in those days, they could not have celebrated the jayanti or taken out processions. I sensed a new confidence amongst the lower-caste students after the performance of this play, and, as the days passed they seemed to realize that if there could be no boundaries at school, perhaps it was true that they had after all been created equal. It was a turning point for the rest of the village too, and to their credit, there was no fuss about the play or the fact that the children were studying together with none of the traditional boundaries between them. I think it helped that behind both the play and the school were a couple with no ulterior motives; no political agendas. A husband and wife who lived with them and seemed to want the same thing all parents do: a better world for their children.

‘the real hero is a heroine’

It was a strange twist of fate: my school now meant the little children of Deora no longer had to walk those 12 kilometres to Itaunja, but every time my wife wanted to go to her parents’ house, she had to trudge all that way to catch a bus to Lucknow. It was hard for her, especially by the winter of 1972, because Nirmala was now pregnant. I would walk with her and try to keep her in good humour, but the distance could not be reduced. Once in a while, a bullock cart would trundle past and Principal Sahiba would get a lift to Itaunja, but the bullock carts were uncomfortable too.

By the time summer came around, Nirmala was heavily pregnant and I would hope each time we set out that there would be a rickshaw or a horse cart to take her to the Itaunja bus stand, but usually none were available. On one occasion, on the way back, the horse cart in which my pregnant wife was sitting toppled over and she fell on to the road. Miraculously, she and our two unborn boys escaped unhurt. On another occasion, she slipped and fell into a drain and cried all the way home, she now tells me. Then there was the time when she was walking to our school alone when a black cobra appeared before her. However, rather than lunging at her it froze and wrapped itself up into a tight coil. Ever after, the villagers narrated this incident as proof of the ancient old wives' tale that a poisonous snake would be struck blind if it looked at a pregnant woman.

Meanwhile, I was experiencing labour pains of my own. I needed government recognition if I was to get public funds for my school. My school would, however, only be recognized if it was run by a registered charitable society.

Therefore, in March 1973, we formed a registered society with Professor R.C. Misra, my teacher from university, as founder-president and me as founder-manager. The other founder members included Nirmala and Bali. The society was named Bharatiya Gramin Vidyalaya (Indian Village School), and the school was designated the same name. I could hardly believe it. That one room we had built with our own hands had a name; an official existence. It wasn't just a shed with windows, but was about to become a school in the eyes of the Government of Uttar Pradesh.

In April 1973, the ninth month of Nirmala's pregnancy, she went for her confinement to her parents' home in Lucknow. I was quite complacent because her doctor had said she was due only in the second week of May, but on the afternoon of 4 May she went into labour. A senior midwife, Misrain Chachi, was called. She examined my wife, I am told, and, behind Nirmala's back, raised two fingers. Everyone in the room now knew what my wife still did not: there were two children coming.

There were no sonograms in those days, at least not where we lived, and even her doctor in Lucknow was more a general practitioner than an OB/GYN. Misrain Chachi had handled scores of deliveries, and had in fact helped to deliver most of Nirmala's siblings. This time, however, she said it was too complicated: not only was my wife having twins, one of them was breached. Nirmala was rushed to Queen Mary's Hospital, only to be turned away. The doctors at Queen Mary's were on one of those periodic strikes that still cripple the medicare system across India.

By now, she was in agonizing pain. She was taken to Duffrin Hospital, where she was finally handed over to a doctor, but the latter, incredibly, was more irritated than concerned: a complicated delivery could mean hours and she had just completed her shift. Nirmala was all alone by now, her relatives having been asked to wait outside. However, rather than treat her or ease her pain, my wife's trauma was worsened by extremely rough treatment at the doctor's hands, and the worst was yet to come.

When the doctor realized the delivery could take all night, she just turned on her heels and headed home, leaving terrified Nirmala crying on the delivery table. One of the nurses felt sorry for her and thankfully gave her moral support through the night and eventually performed the delivery.

All this while, I was oblivious of Nirmala's predicament, at the happy celebration of a thread ceremony in Deora. A feast had been organized, and there was a live band. All of a sudden, the band left the house where the young boy had just been initiated into the Brahminical order, and began playing at my door. That was how I found out I was the father of two boys: someone had brought the news from Lucknow.

Congratulations began pouring in for our family, and *bakshish* stacked for the band people. In an hour, I believe, my two boys had earned more gifts for the band people than the teen for whom the band had been officially performing.

I didn't wait for any of that. As soon as I heard, I proceeded to Lucknow on foot. I was walking quite fast, reached Itaunja, and boarded a bus. When I reached Lucknow and met my wife in the afternoon of 5 May 1973, she was lying on the hospital bed with our babies by her side. As soon as she saw me, she began sobbing, and I didn't even know why. I only found out how badly she had been treated much later, when she told me in her childlike way that she hoped her two sons would grow up, return to the hospital, and beat up the doctor. Two days later, my wife finally left that dreadful hospital and returned to her parents' home.

May and June passed off quite peacefully. School was shut for the summer, so we could focus on our new babies. Two of my wife's younger sisters, Guddi (Sushma) and Beeno (Beena) helped take care of the babies in Lucknow, and once we were back in Deora, two of my stepsisters, Rampati and Kokila, helped my wife. My wife's greatest source of strength in those days was, however, her mother, who had raised six children by herself and was not in the least bit phased by the two noisy boys and their constant squeals for attention. Eventually, we settled into a routine back home in Deora, just my wife, my sons, and I, but it was still sometimes very overwhelming for Nirmala.

At night, she would sleep with one son on either side while I slept on a *charpai* nearby. When one of the boys wet the bed and began crying, my wife would begin changing his clothes, but invariably the other one would wet the bed too and both of them would be crying at the same time. Often, my exhausted Nirmala would give up and cry with them. I would then wake up and take one baby in my arms while my wife changed the other's clothes. Finally, all three would be peacefully asleep again.

When school reopened in July, Nirmala would leave our babies in the mud house at Deora, come to school with me at 7 a.m., complete her role as Principal Sahiba and return at 1 p.m. to the village to feed the babies and eat something herself.

In August, we celebrated the 'Annaprasan' (cereal ceremony) of little Neelesh and Shailesh, who were finally eating solids. Now the children could eat while their mother was away and the strain on Nirmala lessened. By this time, however, the stress had already taken its toll. In the third week of August, my wife developed a high fever, acute weakness, and would not eat anything. There was no doctor around to consult and I was beginning to get frantic. I thought of my mother and all the stories I'd heard of her sudden illness and rapid deterioration.

Desperate, I sent a message to the compounder in the next village, Harinarain Singh. He arrived the following morning, gave her an injection and a few medicines and my wife was better almost instantly. I wonder whether that was all that would have been necessary to save my mother. Perhaps she would have lived a long life once she had got past that illness. She might even have lived to see my two boys and help my wife look after them.

During his next visit, I asked Harinarain Singh about the ailment. He said it was calcium fever. My wife had been feeding two children and needed more calcium than she was getting. After that, I determined to take better care of her and ensure she was eating properly and getting enough rest.

It had been just a year since we opened our school, and the change was already visible in Deora. The children had begun to organize their own plays and singing competitions on special occasions, and this had brought life to our otherwise dull village. On Independence Day, 1973, we arranged a wrestling competition and sports meet for the day and, in the evening, a play entitled *Raja Harishchandra* (The Truthful King). The mini fete drew a huge crowd from a number of villages around Deora, and at the end of the day, everyone even went home with a message about the importance of truthfulness, courtesy the play. Two months later, our students organized a Ram Lila performance, a re-enactment of the life of Lord Rama. It was a big draw and became an annual event in our village for several years. Badlu of Deora made *maur* and *jhalar* (decorative fringe hanging on doors) and Ravana out of paper for our Ram Lila programme.

Nirmala and I were thrilled at the early results of our efforts, but we sometimes felt we were not doing our sons justice by keeping them in the village. There was still no electricity there, or even proper kerosene lamps. The weather was either sweltering hot with no fan and occasional showers that leaked through the thatched roof, or freezing cold with no heater. If the boys fell ill, there was nothing to save them other than village herbs and *totka* (witchcraft). There were also scorpions and snakes lurking in the mud walls and we lived in constant terror that our babies would be stung.

By the following year, the number of students in our school had risen to 150, but there was still no money forthcoming. Our personal expenses had also risen after the birth of our sons and we were still not making anything from my agricultural land. As my savings from Canada dwindled, we realized that we would have to choose between shutting the school or taking up jobs to support it.

As a sort of middle path, my wife and I decided that one of us should take up a job and the other one should try and keep the school going. As I would earn more as a geologist than she would as a teacher or principal, we decided I should look for work.

In response to a circular for recruitment, I went to the Directorate of Geology and Mining in Madhya Pradesh in early 1974. There, I was interviewed by D.B. Asthana (director) and Professor Aswathanarayan of Sagar University (expert). Professor Aswathanarayan told me he had heard of my research work. He was a little surprised, he added, that I was applying for a job at such a low grade. I told him about how I had left Canada to return to my village and build my dream school. He looked a bit puzzled, but I got the job.

I returned to Lucknow and consulted my former teacher, Professor R.C. Misra, and my father-in-law, both of whom advised me to accept the offer. Though I would be earning quite well, the job meant I would be posted in Raipur. It felt like a double exile, from my wife and sons and from all civilization: the area where I was being sent was deep in the jungles of Madhya Pradesh.

A few days before I left, I went to see the school for what might perhaps be the last time. As I was leaving, I remember telling my wife, I stopped and looked back and it was almost as if I was saying goodbye. My wife tried to comfort me, and said the school would not be closed down. I was not equally sanguine.

I should have known better. My wife rose to the challenge like an epic heroine, as my friend V.V.N. Simharao likes to say. 'No doubt you, Shiva Balak Misra, are the hero of this story,' he would tell me, 'but the real hero is a heroine, Nirmala Shukla. She took everything in her stride, faced the roughest weather and stood by the project to bring it to the present state.'

I missed my sons' first birthday while I was in Raipur. I believe it was quite a celebration, with a party organized in their honour at my in-laws' home. Rather than blowing out a candle and cutting a cake, however, they had a more traditional ceremony involving two glasses of milk and a *lota* (small metallic pitcher) full of water covered with an earthen *dweep* or oil lamp representing Ganesha, the God of Wisdom.

My wife and children spent most of May and part of June 1974 at my in-laws' home. The second half of June would however prove a challenge for Nirmala. The academic year was set to start the following month and, while caring for her sons, she had to also ensure that the village folk did not lose heart now that I was gone, and stop sending their children to our school.

While she was well known and very well liked in Deora, Nirmala was still a stranger, and an outsider, in the surrounding villages. She didn't however let that stop her. For two weeks, she travelled from village to village, taking one or two women or a teacher along, to ensure that everyone understood that classes at the school would continue as usual.

To keep the school alive, she told them, they could donate some grain out of their small produce towards the school's expenses. Nirmala later told me she felt the villagers might take education more seriously, and feel they had a greater stake in the school, if they made even the most meagre contribution to its finances, in whatever way they could. I think her ploy worked. People did seem to take the school more seriously once they were paying for their children to attend, even though that (totally voluntary) payment was just a handful of wheat or rice.

Throughout the early days of her campaigning, however, Nirmala ran into a subtle issue of protocol: she invariably got taken in for tea by hordes of womenfolk when what she really wanted to do was to talk to the decision-makers, the men. Finally, after walking for hours in the scorching sun only to be ushered into a courtyard yet again by groups of chattering women, she hit upon a plan. From the next day onwards, she would go to the house of one of the farmers in the village and ask him to assemble the rest. Then the school and our efforts, and the importance of education were discussed and the schoolgoing children were counted and their names duly noted. The business of the day completed, she would then gladly join the women for the mandatory tea and snacks.

Sometimes, the farmers would pay their 'fee' of grain on the spot. On other occasions, my wife would leave the village with a promise from the farmers to send their children to the school the following month. Invariably, Nirmala would urge the villagers to send their girls to school as well. Look at me, she would tell them. I am the principal of your school and I am running it alone. What makes you doubt that your girls are capable of anything less?

i conduct a wedding ceremony

My first posting after I left Deora was Chauraiya, a remote, dacoit-infested village, home to a few scattered forest-dwellers. This was the domain of dacoit Moorat Singh and, just as I had seen in the Hindi films, villagers here would glance about furtively before even uttering his name. Dacoits had clearly demarcated areas of operation in those days, and well-built, well-trained henchmen to do their bidding. In fact, these gangs were the primary source of employment for young men in the more unruly Indian states, much as drug-runners and those trafficking in women are, I believe, in Harlem.

Chauraiya was breathtakingly beautiful: a few mud huts in a lush valley with green hills rising on all sides and a little river running through. The nearest bus stand, police station, and the main road were, however, 20 kilometres away. Two geologists were already working at the camp in Chauraiya when I arrived: Suresh Tandon from Rewa and a certain Beohar from Jabalpur. I had come from Raipur.

The Directorate of Geology and Mining had regional headquarters at Raipur, Jabalpur, Rewa, Gwalior, and Bhopal. The man in charge of the regional headquarters at Gwalior was pudgy Modghare. When I joined, there was a hilarious story doing the rounds about him. Apparently, Modghare had had quite a few run-ins with the previous director, Harishchandra, who was extremely stern and very bad-tempered. The director would yell at Modghare nearly every day, and the poor man could never utter a word in response because he was junior. Therefore, to ease his humiliation, the chubby Modghare would stand in front of his mirror before leaving for work every morning and 'have it out' with Harishchandra. 'Haria,' he would shriek (he had even given the director a derogatory nickname), 'I will kill you. Who do you think you are, screaming at people all day? Don't you know everyone hates you? You had better watch out.' Then, Modghare would thump his thighs like an Indian wrestler and say: 'Come on Haria, let's go. Let's fight it out, man to man, if you have the guts.' Modghare would then rush off to work, not wishing tardiness to be added to his long list of flaws, and there he would invariably be forced to stand with head bowed while the director berated him yet again.

One morning, a colleague stopped by Modghare's house to discuss an assignment, and witnessed the astonishing spectacle. Stifling his giggles, he rushed back to the office to tell the others. As the tale spread, it was difficult to tell who was more embarrassed, Modghare or Harishchandra. Either way, the director retired soon after and Modghare finally got a break.

During my first few weeks at Chauraiya, I was the subject of considerable drama myself, though I was totally unaware of it. Apparently, dreaded dacoit Moorat Singh had not taken kindly to government men poking about in his territory with strange-looking equipment and without ever offering him any protection money. He therefore got some of his trusted aides from the village to shadow us while we worked. Not satisfied with their vague reports – the poor men had no real idea what we were doing – he had some of his musclemen infiltrate our camps posing as labourers, and ordered them to report on our daily activities in minute detail. When these reports confirmed that our activities were harmless, and involved no profit, he eventually decided to leave us alone, he cheerfully told my colleague Suresh, who ran into him at the local lock-up after the dreaded dacoit surrendered. Imagine that ... A murderous henchmen in my camp and I totally unaware of it!

Back in Deora, my wife was finding it impossible to take care of both our sons and manage the school. She therefore began leaving one son in Lucknow with her mother and sisters, 'exchanging' the boys every fortnight. There was an upside to this arrangement: both boys got acquainted with both city and village life very early in their lives, and eventually they could both speak fluent Hindi as well as *dehati* (the village dialect).

We like to think they missed their mother, and hopefully their father too, while they were there, but Sushma, Nirmala's sister, tells me they were so well taken care of at Lucknow that they never once cried for either of us.

All this while, it was up to Nirmala to deal with the hassles of running the school. I could not even guide my wife as she had no telephone in Deora. Instead, Nirmala had to depend on letters, which usually took about 10 days each way.

She did, however, have her father to guide her. Before I left, I had asked Shuklaji to act as school manager in my absence. He remained in this position until his death in 1998. It was during his tenure as manager that the school got temporary recognition in 1974, and permanent recognition in 1982.

My first month in Churaiya was quite memorable. Not only was I shadowed by a dreaded dacoit's henchmen but also officiated (for the first and assuredly the last time) as a Brahmin priest at a wedding. It was 10 p.m. and I had turned for the night to my tent when an elderly man rushed in, pleading with me to perform his daughter's wedding. 'But I don't know how,' I started, grabbing my dressing gown and wrapping it over my pyjamas. Brushing aside this minor detail, the man wailed that I had to help him; had to help his daughter who was all dressed up and waiting to be married. Then, without warning, he dropped to the ground and lay prostrate at my feet in entreaty. 'But why,' I asked him, considerably alarmed, 'and why me?'

The pundit he had engaged, the man told me, had gone off to perform another wedding where he had been offered more money. The groom's family, meanwhile, had arrived at the village and if they returned, he wailed, his daughter 'would surely be sentenced to a lifetime of loneliness'. He came close to me, and murmured that he had come to me because some of the labourers working at the camp had told him I was a Brahmin and might help.

I was quite disgusted with the mercenary pundit and felt quite sorry for the poor man, so I asked him what needed to be done. If the entrance ceremony or *dwar* puja was performed, he said, the groom's family would not go back. That sounded within my reach, having seen some *dwar* pujas performed in my village, but then I remembered that the rituals varied from region to region. I asked the father of the bride if there were any local details I should be aware of. It's a good thing I asked. Apparently, one of the rituals in Chauraiya included the groom hurling a broom into the bride's house, an event I am certain would have quite unsettled me had I not been prepared for it.

All set, I donned my dhoti and kurta and marched to the house, clutching a thick diary masquerading as a prayer book. When we got to his door, I loudly ordered the man to fetch the *thali* (metal plate) with the puja items: grains of rice, turmeric powder, betel leaves, and spices. Hearing my voice, the guests gathered reverently for the puja. I began chanting, loudly and confidently, throwing flowers and grains of rice at the guests every now and again, but soon I had pretty much run out of shlokas. I wasn't sure what to do next, so I just started all over again, peeking from the corner of my eye to see if anyone had noticed.

Other than the glowering groom, everyone seemed to be quite satisfied with my service and were going about their business as usual, discussing the bride's outfit, gossiping about the dowry, and deciding who would make a good match for whom. In between, I asked the old man to garland the groom and the father of the groom. Then I solemnly asked the groom to throw the broom. The *dwar* puja completed, I rushed off the dais before the bride's father got any ideas. The man was effusive in his thanks and, before he dropped to the ground again, I decided to return to my tent to catch up with some sleep. The marriage proper was eventually performed early in the morning, I discovered later, by the same pundit, on his way back from the more lucrative assignment.

I still wonder whether I should have refused to perform the puja. After all, I was not ordained, but being ordained had not uplifted the priest's soul very much. Besides, I like to think that God has a sense of humour about such things.

***

Not long after my one-night stint as a Brahmin priest, my sons had an important puja of their own: the *mundan* ceremony or first shaving of the head. This is generally a big event in Hindu families. However, as I was away, my wife organized a simple ceremony. The *mundan* was performed near a *mazar* or shrine about half a kilometre south of Deora, by one of the Muslim barbers from my village. All the women from the village gathered and sang the special songs for the occasion and there was a feast in the evening. Laddoos were distributed to all the villagers.

I don't know how Nirmala paid for all this: I had not received a salary in three months, and I had not even been able to take leave to go to Lucknow and withdraw money from my bank. Thankfully, I completed my field-work at Chauraiya soon after my sons' *mundan*, and when I returned to our regional office at Raipur, my salary slip had finally arrived. I immediately wrote to my wife to take a break and join me in Raipur for a brief vacation.

I still remember pacing up and down the platform at the railway station, waiting to see my little family again. Suddenly there they were, Nirmala striding along, with one son's fist held firmly in each hand, and an overburdened coolie barely able to stand under the weight of their luggage. That was Nirmala all right. She never went anywhere without an outfit for every imaginable occasion. Why is it, I still cannot fathom, that women must pack virtually everything they own even if they're just going off for the weekend? Well, luggage or not, it was good to see Nirmala again.

We spent a couple of weeks at Raipur and returned together to Lucknow to celebrate Holi. Immediately after the festivities were over, I had to return to work, but my family could come along this time. Nirmala could go during preparation leave in the school. Don't leave on the first day after Holi, my father-in-law warned. It's not an auspicious day to set out. How quaint, I thought. The old man is superstitious. I have to return to work, I laughed. I had exhausted my leave, and we had train reservations. Well, it was March 1975 and, as I would soon discover, perhaps we should have listened to my father-in-law.

It started as soon as I got back to the head office. Some jealous colleague, I discovered, had told the director, D.B. Asthana, that I had gone on leave without notifying anyone. The director, not as stern as bad-tempered Harishchandra, but a man who could clearly distinguish right from wrong, was hopping mad. I had just joined, he pointed out; what did I mean by running off without a word?

I rushed back to my desk and returned with an envelope containing my letter of application, which I had duly handed over to a colleague, and the acknowledgment and sanction he had received from my immediate superior. Well, that was the end of that. Quite unnerving, I thought, but hardly what one would call a curse. Little did I realize?

That evening, while my wife was cooking dinner on a kerosene stove her cotton sari caught fire from the *angithi* kept on the floor behind her. The flames had eaten through several layers of the thin cloth by the time she realized what had happened. I suddenly heard her scream and rushed to the kitchen, where I saw her thrashing about in flames. I snatched the first thing that came to hand, a small bucket of water we kept just outside the kitchen, and doused the flames. She was thankfully unhurt, but there was more to follow.

Within the week, I received orders from the director to head to Bailadilla, famous for malaria and mosquitoes, to scout for iron-ore deposits. With two little children and a wife in tow, it was a frightening prospect, but we decided to go and check it out. Soon after we arrived, little Shailesh caught malaria. He had a raging fever and had to be admitted to a hospital, where he was constantly injected, tested, and fed dreadful-tasting medicines by the nurses. The poor child was so tortured, that the mere sight of a woman in white would set him bawling.

Despite all the treatment, Shailesh's malaria continued to rage. Eventually, we decided that Nirmala and the children should return to Raipur or Lucknow, where there were better hospitals and less chances of relapse of the high fever. I think the gods finally decided we had suffered enough, because by the time we got to Lucknow, the circuit was complete and the post-Holi curse had lifted.

When I returned to Raipur after seeing my family safely settled into Nirmala's parents' home once again, I received a letter bearing the glorious news that I had been transferred to Rewa. I was the happiest man on earth, because Rewa was so close to Lucknow that my wife and children could come and join me whenever they wished.

In Rewa, I rented a spacious house belonging to a certain Rau from Chitrakoot, a very small state during British times. Then I wrote to my wife to convey the good news to her, and was surprised when she didn't respond. Perhaps she was busy preparing for the next school year, I thought, but she should at least have written back. On 5 June 1975 (I still remember the date) I was in the kitchen of my large house in Rewa, making a lonely cup of tea and wondering whether my wife would get used to not having me around, when I suddenly heard the squeals of my boys, now two years old.

My wife had decided to surprise me, so she had come all the way to Rewa on her own, following the directions I had provided in my letter. She had changed trains at Allahabad and then caught a bus at a chaotic terminus, with two little boys and, of course, what appeared to be all her worldly belongings. As my toddlers clambered all over me in greeting, I marvelled at the quiet strength of this woman. I thought to myself once again of how right Bacchu had been all those years ago when he first told me that he had this cousin, and he thought she and I would make a great match.

the village of change

In Kunaura, our school's finances were looking up after we got temporary recognition from the government in 1974. One teacher's salary was now paid for by the state, and we were being reimbursed for the fees of all the scheduled caste students in our school. The teachers were still receiving only meagre salaries, but their dedication was phenomenal and they even looked after the administration of the school for a few days every now and again, allowing my wife to take a break and visit me in the field.

In 1977, I was assigned the jungles of the tribal Bastar area for geological investigation. By now, I was getting tired of living alone, missing watching my sons grow up. I had packed my bags and was waiting alone for the jeep to take me from my lovely house in Rewa to the wilderness of Bastar when it hit me like a wave: what was the point of it all? What was the point of pouring your whole life and all your time into your work, putting it before everything else? This wasn't life.

Life was what I had left behind, and by the time I got back, I might have missed the best of it.

Then, sitting in the central courtyard of the big house, dejection, I must admit, turned to melodrama. Here you are, all packed up and leaving everything behind once again, I told myself, and the office jeep hasn't even arrived to uproot you. The truth is, the jeep was eventually over a day late, and as I sat there on my holdall, waiting, I wrote a fairly morose poem: '*Meri zindagi bhi koi zindagi hai, akela musafir chala jaa raha hoon* (Is this any sort of life to lead, a lone wanderer forever journeying alone).' Feeling extremely sorry for myself, I unpacked a few essentials. It was evening and the jeep would eventually arrive the next day. Had I known what Bastar was going to be like, I think I would have written a far more soulful poem.

Let me first describe the tribals' diet (it won't take long): rice, meat, and toddy; that was it. This was worse than Canada, for at least in the latter there were berries and small animals! Vegetables and dal were a distant dream. The only real solace for me was that my tribal cook knew how to make chapatis and parathas. In addition to my cook with his limited skills, there were five tribal attendants, a driver, and a watchman at the camp. If life in Bastar was difficult, winning the trust of the local tribals was even more challenging. They were forever standing around in the marketplace in groups, glaring at us, and whispering about how we were trying to take over their land.

Once a group of tribals stopped us and shouted: 'These mountains and jungles are ours. Why are you roaming around doing tring-tring [the sound of the hammer on rocks, I imagine]? We worship them and you disturb them even without offering a chicken to the Gods.' I tried to explain to them that, as a Brahmin, I could offer no such sacrifice to their gods as it went against the rules of my own: oh dear, I thought, why was I always running into such dreadful carnivores? It was just as if one of the tribals had read my mind. He raised his arm ever so slightly and I noticed he was carrying a bow and arrow, all ready to shoot, it would appear. I decided to end the debate over the chicken sacrifice and get moving. 'Come on, let's go,' I ordered my men in as commanding a voice as I could muster. Out of the corner of my eye, I saw the man lower his arrow and breathed a sigh of relief.

The tribals however had us scared for a while. Some of the officials working in the area, including a malaria inspector, a local teacher, and government security guard began insisting that we sacrifice a chicken to appease the tribals, if not their gods. 'Go ahead, sir, your gods will understand,' the watchman would reason, nodding his head sagely. Nothing doing, I said; if they wanted to give the tribals their sacrifice, they'd have to find another geologist. I would not succumb to blackmail. I wasn't about to officiate in a ritual that still seems to me nothing short of barbaric, just because my colleague were unable to stare down a few local people.

Other than the urge to wring a chicken's neck, the tribals of Bastar were simple and honest people. There was virtually no crime here, and you could leave the most expensive equipment lying around and no one would touch it. Touch one of their women, though, and you were done for. There was a story going around that a government official had once tried to rape a young tribal girl. Her entire clan got together to drag the man into the forests, then buried him neck-deep in the earth and force-fed him some poisonous concoction. They then formed a circle around him and danced, drank, and chanted till he died early next morning.

I, frankly, had no problem with their system of instant justice, but I just could not get used to their food. In addition to meat and toddy, they loved to eat a nauseating paste of red ants. In fact, if we were walking in the forest and they noticed a nest of red ants, they would refuse to go a step further until they had taken all the ants with them. They also loved bidis and their faces would light up if you offered them one. They loved cockfights too, and in every market, at every festival, and on every occasion or gathering, there had to be a cockfight. Rumour had it that one of the ministers in Pandit Jawaharlal Nehru's cabinet, a tribal from the same region, flew all the way back to his village to watch the finals of the annual cock-fighting championship. Going by the hysteria each match generated, I could well believe that.

I was myself quite drawn into it too. I found it intriguing to watch the two birds battle it out, and then watch the agony of the man who's fowl had lost and the ecstatic grin of the other as he picked up both birds and took then home, the one undoubtedly to be pampered, and the other to be chopped up and roasted.

In Bastar, once I stayed at a tiny village guesthouse with mud walls, set on open ground near a primary school: a tent would not have been safe because the village was in the midst of dense jungle and there were a lot of wild animals about. The school had one teacher, whom I never saw, and rarely any students.

It did have something I would subsequently petition the government for myself: the promise of little bowls of porridge for students who stayed till lunch time. Imagine that, I marvelled. Students rewarded just for turning up. I thought of our school kids and the long distances some of them walked to get to our school at Kunaura. So many more might be allowed to come, I remember thinking, if their parents knew there was a free meal to be had.

At the guesthouse, the village watchman had told me very firmly that I should always keep a fire burning outside the front door. I didn't know why, and I didn't intend to follow an old man's odd advice, so I didn't ask. Then, on one full moon night, the fire had died out and my wife had gone to the toilet behind the building. Suddenly, I heard a shriek and she came darting back indoors. An angry looking man in a dhoti and undershirt had come striding towards her, she said. Then our watchman came along, doing his rounds and banging his stick, and the man just vanished. Some weeks later, one of the villagers told me that the guesthouse was haunted, and the doorway should always be lit by a fire to keep the spirits at bay. The next time an old man gave me advice, I decided, I would at least ask him why.

* * *

In May 1977, when my sons were four, I got them admitted to a school in Rewa. I still remember the expression on their little faces on the first day – somewhere between anxiety and excitement. As I turned away, Shailesh followed me quietly out of the class, as if he had already had enough. He went right back in when I ordered him to, but he looked very hurt and abandoned. Neelesh, on the other hand, was already making friends. On the second day, I asked Neelesh: 'So, how's it going?' 'I have a best friend in my class,' he grinned. 'What's your best friend's name?' I asked. Navita Gulati, he replied: he had made friends with the daughter of a famous doctor at Rewa Hospital. Well, that was how my boys were: Shailesh always the shy one, Neelesh a ladies' man (and proud of it) right from the very outset.

Now that my sons were in school, I was determined to find a more stable job, and one that didn't entail my having to move from camp to camp all the time and where I could look after my sons while my wife was managing the school. I thought back to my peaceful days as a teacher and decided to try for a job in that profession. Sometime in early 1978, I wrote to Professor K.S. Valdiya, one of my teachers at Lucknow University and now the head of the geology department at Kumaun University in Nainital. He suggested I join him as research associate, with the aim of becoming a lecturer at the earliest opportunity.

The offer was purely a temporary assignment, but I decided to take it anyhow in the interest of my boys. I resigned from my government post, astonishing many of my friends that I was giving up the job security and fringe benefits that it had brought, and joined Valdiya's research project. Now that we were settled, Nirmala and I could also think of taking our social work to the next level. We had been discussing for a while how we would like to promote socio-economic programmes like adult education and dairy farming; and, for the women, tailoring and food-processing. An additional income to the families of poor farmers would improve their children's nutrition, their clothing, and capacity to pay fees.

It was around this time that Nirmala was selected to be sent to America for a social training programme in America. Her name was proposed by Urmila Devi and Kamle Gupta of the Agricultural Extension Department at the Bakshi-ka-Talab development block. My friend Simharao, who was in Lucknow at the time, was adamant that she accept the offer. She, for her part, was in two minds because her going to America would probably mean we would have to shut down our school, and of course it meant Neelesh and Shailesh would be left without a mother for two years.

She wrote to ask me what she should do. I didn't reply. The truth is, I didn't know how to respond to her. The last date for submission of her letter of acceptance passed and that was the end of an opportunity for a career for Nirmala.

***

Nainital, with its huge freshwater lake, lush greenery, and cool, pleasant weather was a stark contrast with dusty, scorching Bastar, Raipur, and Rewa.

In the first week of May 1978 I went to Nainital to see it for myself. When I got down from the taxi at Tallital bus stand and stood facing the lake, I was overwhelmed. This is where my sons should live and grow up, I thought to myself. I decided to visit the Kumaun University right away, but locating it proved more difficult than finding Memorial University in St John's, Newfoundland.

I asked someone how I could get there, and he guided me to what is known as Sleepy Hollow. I had to ask several people along the way and they all had the same answer. I reached there after walking 2 kilometres to find it was the administrative building. This was 'university' to the local people. 'Where is the geology department,' I asked someone in the administrative building. He asked me to go to D.S.B. Degree College. I walked back over Ayarpatta hill and eventually met Professor Valdiya. I discussed my plan to come to Nainital and join on 14 May 1978.

There were just 30,000 people living in the city in those days. The air was fresh, roads easy to walk on, virtually no automobiles. In summer, however, during the tourist season, the population jumped to about a lakh. I moved there during the tourist season and was astonished to find that once the summer ended over half the people disappeared altogether.

Professor K.S. Valdiya was conducting a research project on the Nainital hills, to be completed in about three years. He was a very warm and affectionate man and seemed quite fond of me and my family: he would call Nirmala 'Sita Maiya' and the boys Luv and Kush after the wife and twin boys of our Hindu epic hero Rama.

The geology department at Kumaun University was on the southern edge of the Ayarpatta hill, adjacent to the clear, blue lake. It was a small department, with just three teachers: Dr R.N. Pande, Dr Arun Kumar, Dr V.N. Agrawal, who later moved to Brazil, and Dr Valdiya besides one or two research students.

I checked into Himalaya Hotel and began to look for a house: the next academic year was about to begin and I was in a hurry to bring my boys over and get their names registered into a good school. Thankfully, one of the teachers in my department, Dr Arun Kumar (a former student of mine at Kanya Kubja Degree College in Lucknow), had a suite available in the house he had rented. I gladly accepted this accommodation in the house of Pooran Chand Bhatt, at a monthly rental of Rs 175.

In the last week of June, I brought my family to Nainital. My brother-in-law, Surendra Nath Shukla, now a leading IT professional, also came to live with us and took admission in the B.Sc. course in July, with geology as one of the subjects.

I got my sons admitted to Class I at a school right next door. Nainital being peaceful and safe, my sons could walk to class every morning with Neeraj, the landlord's son and their classmate. However, it was difficult after Nirmala returned to Lucknow, with me now having to fulfil the role of two parents. We had no full-time help, so I was waking up at the crack of dawn, fixing breakfast and getting the boys ready for school, lecturing all day and returning home in the evening to cook for the boys and to help them with their homework. It's a good thing my brother-in-law Surendra was around or I think, I would have lost my mind. I no longer scoff when people say housework is among the hardest, and loneliest, of jobs.

We had a maid to do the cleaning, but having Sushila trawling through the house brought problems of its own. She used to call our house *dhungani* or heap of stones because I was always bringing rock samples home from the Nainital hills to study. 'I keep cleaning up and you keep bringing more mud and dirt into the house,' she would scold. 'You should know better how to keep the house clean ...'

One day I had taken out my four precious fossil specimens from Canada to study and left them on the table. This was apparently too much for her. She swept up the 'creepy stones', as she described them to me later, and threw them outside in the trash! A couple of hours later, I got back to the table to find them gone. I was searching frantically and was about to shout at the boys and remind them that my work material was not to be played with, when she sheepishly confessed what she had done. I rushed out and found them safe in their plastic bag, but I warned her, in a quivering voice, that the next time she touched the 'creepy stones' she would have to find herself another job.

I was now just an overnight train journey away from Nirmala and our school, and Nirmala even had a telephone connection in her father's house, so I could now spend all my time off and the school holidays with my family and our project. We now had agricultural extension programmes organized at our school with the help of the Agricultural Extension Department of the local development block. Indeed, even my dream of a midday porridge snack for our students had become a reality.

CARE was providing raw porridge for pre-primary students through the Education Department and Nirmala had signed us up. That programme was discontinued in 1978, but that very year Nirmala found a similar scheme funded by the central government and applied on behalf of our students. Our school was accepted into the programme and, for the next four years, the government also paid out a sum of Rs 50 per month for a teacher, Rs 25 for a helper, and 30 paise per day per child for refreshments.

Around that time, the central government also began a course for dropout adult girls and semi literate women, which our school society signed up for, under Nirmala's leadership. It was hugely effective in the field of adult education for women. The first centre was at Amaniganj, where I had gone to school as a little boy. Under the adult education programme, 25 women were paid a stipend of Rs 25 per month to study. Tuition and even textbooks were free. The women attended regular classes for two years, and 80 per cent of them then passed the matriculation examination. The following year, more women signed up, and even the sceptics changed their tune when the results came in: again, 80 per cent had passed. Nirmala, as coordinator of the centres, made the sessions lively and fun, just as she had first done with our village women and schoolchildren. She organized cultural shows and creative activities like painting, knitting, and singing competitions.

It had taken many years, but I could now see in Deora the change I had so naively expected to see on my return from Canada. The women who had passed school through the adult education programme now came forward to teach others. Many of them got jobs as instructors in *balwadis* and *aanganwadis* (government-run schools and creches). When I returned to Deora for the first time after moving to Nainital, it seemed so bustling and alive; as if hope had finally arrived. I thought back to the fancy penthouse in Ottawa, where I had decided to return to my dark village; thought of the first year of my marriage, with Nirmala wading to school in knee-high floodwater, clutching a change of clothes; and felt blessed to have played a role in what I saw before me. If we hadn't done it, someone else would have; eventually. How blessed that we should have been the chosen ones.

bringing up the kids, suing a journalist

I was very happy working as a teacher in the geology department of Kumaun University, teaching economic geology and mineral exploration. I would, of course, have much rather been teaching precambrian geology. Doing that, I could have opened up the textbooks and pointed to photographs I had taken of the 565-million-year-old fossils that I had discovered in Canada! Curiously, the rocks of the Nainital hills were more or less the same age as those in Newfoundland. They made for a very interesting study.

My sons too had settled well in their new school in class one, although I think their understanding of the history of the struggle for independence of our country was confusing them somewhat. One day, on their way home, little Neelesh and Shailesh saw some white men outside a hotel. Horrified that the British oppressors they had heard such terrible tales about should still be roaming on the streets, they began shouting, perhaps to raise an alarm about the imminent invasion.

'What are they doing here,' Shailesh demanded. 'They have been thrown out of our country by Gandhiji.'

They came home all aflutter, asking why no one had swooped down on the colonialists. I had to gently explain that every white man was not an Englishman ... and that it was not illegal for an Englishman to walk the streets of India. That calmed them down.

In March 1979 was our first Holi festival in Nainital. Nirmala spent days preparing all kinds of sweets for Holi Milan or the ceremonial greeting of friends and neighbours. People came by in the morning to play colours, and went away. We waited all afternoon for them to return for the *milan*, but no one turned up. We learnt later that the sweets should have been offered in the morning, because that's when the festival ended for them. How horrified we were! How rude they must have thought us, we joked, when they dropped by and were not offered so much as a *mithai* (sweetmeat) in greeting.

Back in school, Nirmala had succeeded in obtaining temporary recognition in 1974, and through the late 1970s she and I had been struggling to obtain permanent recognition. For this to happen, we needed to have a concrete building and trained teachers. We had laid the foundation of one concrete room, but in 1976, our financial situation had deteriorated so greatly that we had to sell the bricks of the foundation for money. We did not wish to see our dream project recognized through the oft-used system of bribes and fake certificates, and there was no money available to build the mandatory three rooms measuring 25 ft x 20 ft each, so we decided to wait.

In 1980, my friend Simharao came from Hyderabad to visit me during my winter vacation. He told me he had located Dr Birendra Sahai, one of our friends from the Ottawa penthouse. Sahai had returned to India and was working at the Indian Institute of Technology in Kanpur, just a few hours away by train. Simha and I decided to go there and meet him. While we were there, we also met his colleagues, Professor A.S.R. Sai and Dr Prashant Kumar. The five of us got talking and Sahai told them how I had just upped and left one day to fulfil my dream of building a little school in my village.

The two professors seemed very taken by the story and wanted to hear all about the project. When I finished telling them about the school, with its ups and downs and how we were still waiting and hoping for government recognition, the kind men offered to help. Dr Sai said he had some forty pre-fabricated slabs lying as waste in his department, and offered them to us as roofing. I was thrilled. Simha and I transported the slabs by truck from Kanpur, paying Rs 600. I then arranged for bricks and mortar, and we began construction.

When my vacation ended in February, I returned to Nainital. Simha generously offered to stay on in the village and supervise the work. It was quite a brave thing to offer. Simha didn't know the local dialect, the people of my village knew no English, and each plank, weighing over 100 kilograms, had to be hauled 2 kilometre from Deora to the school. The truck from Kanpur had unloaded them at Deora as it could not transport them to the site where the school was located.

Simha had to negotiate with the villagers for a bullock cart and finally struck a deal with Radheshyam at Rs 2 per slab to be transported. Labour charges per day were another Rs 2, without *pani-patta* (the daily ration of about 100 gm of jaggery and bidis). Simha had no idea what *pani-patta* was, so one day he asked one of the villagers. When he learnt what it was he went out and bought a big chunk of jaggery and distributed it all around, greeting everyone with *'Pani-patta? Pani-patta?'* The labours were thrilled and, forever after, would break out into grins every time they saw him.

Simha was very popular in Deora. The labourers called him Babuji, the villagers called him Junior Engineer. It wasn't much of a designation, but as an official title, it bestowed on him great merit in the field of school-building and gave him the last word in all disputes among the labourers.

Once the walls were up, Simha began to look for oil and paper for pre-fabricating sunshades for the windows. Some oil was traced to the Pradhan or village head of the Ayodhyanagari hamlet near the school, but Simha was just unable to find any paper, he later told me. It was 1980, but there were still no newspapers being delivered to Deora, and in any event few of my fellow villagers would have been able to read them.

* * *

In 1981, the government of Uttar Pradesh announced that all teachers who had completed ten years of service in a recognized school would automatically be considered trained. We, of course, had no such teachers, having obtained temporary recognition of the school only in 1974, but the scheme also offered teachers with five years' experience and the option of completing a correspondence course for the BTC (Basic Teaching Certificate), if they could clear the entrance exam. We now had six teachers, one of them a woman, and they all qualified for the course and then all passed and were certified as teachers the following year. I felt that my dream was coming true: if our teachers had been certified, could the school itself be far behind?

By now, one room was ready, thanks to Simha and Dr Sai. Soon, other friends began coming forward to help keep the construction going. Prashant Kumar pitched in, and we named the room 'Urmila Kaksha', after his mother. Pathik Seva Samiti, a local education trust, provided funds for the remaining rooms. Lo! all of a sudden, we were done. We looked around the neat concrete structure and realized that all the conditions for permanent recognition had been fulfilled. This would make us eligible for government grants called grants-in-aid.

Prabha Kant Shukla was director of Primary Education at this time. Thankfully, he understood the meaning of social work and helped us with a number of issues. I explained to him how the fees for the weaker sections were not being reimbursed by the government, and how the grants for a Sanskrit teacher were not being released. I also told him how the district inspector of schools had taken me off the list because I had refused to pay any bribes. 'All your difficulties...,' the inspector had sneered at me, chewing tobacco as he spoke, 'are because you do not maintain *prabandhakiya* (managerial) relations with the office', whatever that meant!!

The director asked his deputy, Khandelwal, to look into the matter and the dues were finally cleared without any 'managerial relations'.

Shukla also ordered the district inspector of schools and regional director to visit our school and submit a report. Based on their report, the school was given permanent recognition in 1982 and became eligible for grants.

It was difficult to believe, but my sons were now in Class 4, almost through with their primary education. Nirmala wanted them to move to St Joseph's school and my neighbour, Bhavana Shah, a teacher at St Mary's College, kept egging her on. 'Your boys deserve a good school,' she would whisper conspiratorially, as if I wanted to hold my boys back. Then Nirmala would come into the house looking as if all her dreams had been shattered. 'Why won't you go and talk to the principal at least,' she would complain. 'It's your duty to at least try. Why, even Mrs Shah seems to worry more about those boys than you do.'

It wasn't that I didn't want them to go to blessed St Joseph's. It's just that I knew how many children were trying to get in every year, and I was worried that only one of my boys would be admitted, and the other left behind. Finally, hearing how well they had done in Class 4, Mrs Shah came to speak to me herself, and I had to admit she really did seem concerned. I guess the dear woman hadn't just engaged in idle gossip. Well, she ordered me to go and meet Brother Donahue, the principal. Before she joined my wife's chorus about duty and fatherhood, I agreed.

The first thing I saw when I got to the school was a huge notice saying all seats had been filled. Well, I tried, I thought to myself. I went home and told Nirmala to convey my regrets to Mrs Shah, who was over at our house in minutes, insisting that I meet the principal anyway. That woman was over at our house in minutes, insisting that I meet the principal anyway. My wife seemed to have no respect for the sign either and also insisted I go. I was most reluctant, but I figured there was no harm in talking to the man, especially if it would silence them, so off I went again.

'If you have come for admission,' Brother Donahue said as soon as he saw me, 'let me tell you there are no seats left.' I said I had read that on the notice board ... and then stood there, fumbling. What was I supposed to say to the man now, I wanted to ask Mrs Shah? Then, in a rush, I found myself saying things I didn't even know I had been thinking. Growing up in a village with no school I had been fortunate to have been educated in India and abroad, I told Brother Donahue, and I had always dreamt of my children going to a decent school with the best teachers.

'Where did you go abroad?' asked Brother Donahue, suddenly showing some interest for the first time. 'Sir, I went to Canada on a full scholarship,' I said.

Brother Donahue asked me to sit down. 'Where were you in Canada?' he asked. I told him I was at St John's in Newfoundland. It transpired that he had been at St John's too, around the same time, undergoing training for priesthood. We chatted for a long time and Brother Donahue eventually agreed to give my boys admission: both of them. I could hardly believe it. It was only when he asked which class they were in that it actually hit me: Neelesh and Shailesh were going to be St Joseph's boys! I wanted to rush over to Mrs Shah and garland her.

'They have gone to Class 5 in the little school down the road from our house,' I beamed to Brother Donahue, 'but you can put them in any class in which you can accommodate them.' Brother Donahue laughed. 'We will put them in Class 5 but in separate sections,' he said.

* * *

A few months after they joined their new school, Shailesh's class teacher Mrs Menezes called me to complain about his performance. She showed me his incomplete notebook and I was quite upset. 'Yes, I agree with you,' I said. 'He isn't doing sufficiently well and that's a great pity, because his twin brother in the other section is doing excellently.' That's a terrible thing to say, Mrs Menezes said, looking quite stern. 'You must be comparing the two boys all the time, and berating Shailesh.' I had to admit that was exactly what I had been doing. 'It's a natural reaction,' I said. 'Shailesh is just not trying sufficiently hard.' She then showed me some papers where Shailesh had done extremely well. 'Look at these marks,' she said. 'Did you praise him for the effort that went into them?' I had to admit I hadn't. Never compare the two, said Mrs Menezes, and always praise Shailesh when he does well. I guess the poor boy had been feeling demoralized. As soon as I began encouraging him and focusing on his strengths, he generally began doing well in all subjects.

* * *

In 1982, the Central Social Welfare Board announced a dairy scheme for destitute women. We applied on behalf of five such women and the scheme was sanctioned, giving them each an interest-free loan to buy milch cows or buffaloes, which they could then repay in installments from their income. The money was granted to the school as the trustee, so we would buy the animals and hand them over. It was marvellous to watch the women tentatively take the animals home, and later see them confidently marketing the milk and paying the installments on their loans: stable, independent, and successful individuals in their own right. Encouraged by the success of the first round, we arranged for another ten women who also repaid every single paisa to the government. We were extremely happy to be trustees of the project finance.

Another scheme helped train fifty-nine women as seamstresses. It was implemented in two phases, the first at Itaunja (thirty-two women) and the second at Kunaura (twenty-seven women) under Nirmala's supervision. Under this scheme, each woman received Rs 100 per month as a stipend. We helped the trainees to obtain loans from a bank at Itaunja to buy their own sewing machines (at rates also subsidized by the government). All the trainees repaid their loans before their training programme was completed, and many of them found jobs in a matter of days and were able for the first time to take home money they had earned on their own.

Many adult girls and women drop-outs had expressed a desire to continue their education. We found that the Government of India through the Central Social Welfare Board was running a scheme called 'Mahila Condense Course' for backward sections of society or financially needy women. Under the scheme the first centre under the supervision of Nirmala Misra as coordinator was begun at Amaniganj where I had undergone primary education. A batch of twenty-five women and girls was selected. The participating women were required to be taught free, regularly for two years, and at the conclusion of this they appeared for the high school examination. Each woman was given a stipend of Rs 25 per month by the government. The textbooks were free and the examination fee was waived. The first batch in the matriculation examination had a success rate of over 80 per cent. It was commendable that the women beginning as semi-literates could do so well. The second batch was also very successful. These women were infused with hope of a better future for themselves and proved to be torch-bearers of change in the surrounding villages by encouraging others to get educated.

Courses for two more batches of twenty-five women each were conducted at Itaunja from where I had passed the junior High school examination three decades earlier. One of these batches received a visit from Dasgupta, the head of UNICEF for Uttar Pradesh and Bihar, together with the director of child nutrition, Uttar Pradesh, Sushri Chandra Govind. Chandra Govind and an American lady (vice president of UNICEF) had been brought by office of the development block at Bakshi-ka-Talab to show them how we were progressing. The women students at the centres constituted a lively group and the centres became places of cultural and creative activities, such as folk lore, folk dances, singing competitions, knitting, and painting. The women educated through the scheme later volunteered to participate in the socio-economic programmes run either by the school, or by other organizations, or the government. Many of them were employed as instructors in the *balvadis* and *aanganvadis*. A total of eight batches from far-flung places were educated over a period of sixteen years.

Playing a part in these schemes for women was, in some ways, almost more rewarding than the school itself. After all, it's easy to learn when you're a child running to school with the rest of the village children. The women had however been brought up in different times, when all they were expected to do was to have children of their own, preferably not girls. People often scoffed at their efforts, especially initially, holding against them the very illiteracy which the men in their lives had forced upon them. One woman told me, with intense hurt in her eyes, that her husband had laughed at her in front of her son and daughter, both of whom were attending our school. 'What will you study at your age,' he had said. 'Little Sunita going to school is one thing. What do you think you can learn about raising cattle? You can't even write your own name.' Many of the women themselves concurred with this view, even some of those undergoing the training programmes. That however is where the beauty of human nature lies: however often we are told we are worthless, deep down we yearn to prove that is not true.

* * *

At a time when Nirmala was working her fingers to the bone coordinating these programmes and running the school, working up to 10 hours at Kunaura on some days, and then, on other days, rushing to Itaunja and back on foot, a gentleman called Bal Krishna Shrivastava waltzed in and levelled wild accusations against her in print!

Shrivastava, apparently some sort of journalist, visited the training centre at Itaunja in an inebriated state and insisted on talking to the women trainees. Nirmala told him he could not enter the classroom unless he had a relative there, and asked him to talk to the women's families because some of them wore veils and were not permitted to speak to strangers. The man never spoke to their families, or anyone else, and instead wrote a nasty article in an obscure magazine published out of Roorkee, accusing Nirmala of a dictatorial attitude, embezzlement of scholarships, and corruption. This was too much to be ignored and Nirmala was very upset, so I went to my landlord in Nainital, who was a leading lawyer. He drafted a legal notice to the magazine, asking them to publish a rebuttal. However, they did not respond. So Nirmala filed a criminal case of defamation against Shrivastava, the author of the article, and Dr N.R. Goel of Roorkee, who had published it. The case dragged on for over a decade, but the respondents were unable to substantiate any of their allegations. The block development officer of Bakshi-ka-Talab, Surendra Saxena, himself testified to Nirmala's flawless implementation of the scheme, and the fact that he had personally selected all the names for the various programmes.

Eventually, the court found both Shrivastava and Goel guilty of defamation and sentenced them to a year's rigorous imprisonment and a fine of Rs 1,000 each. The correspondent had, however, died in the interim. Goel met Nirmala outside the court after the verdict and politely reminded her that Shrivastava was dead, suggesting that she should perhaps withdraw the case. 'So what if he's dead,' she responded, 'you're alive, aren't you?' Nirmala, never one to be vengeful, had spent sleepless nights worrying about how her reputation had been tarnished. I think the accusations of embezzlement hurt her the most, especially after all the years we had spent pinching pennies, refusing to pay bribes, and denying comforts to our own children to keep our school going. Even had she wished to relent, I think I would have tried to talk her out of it. Soon after the verdict, Goel filed a review petition challenging it, and it remains pending.

a gangster's son becomes a graduate

In the winter of 1987, Simha decided to visit Kunaura on Basant Panchami (believed to be the birthday of Saraswati, the goddess of wisdom). He came all the way from Andhra Pradesh with his friend Narhari, but kept his plan a secret. The two men got to our house at midnight, tired and weary. We were surprised they'd made it alive. They had just travelled through dacoit-infested tracts of Uttar Pradesh, one of the most crime-ridden states in the country, in the dead of night.

The area around Deora was then the domain of Birbal, the crime lord of the nearby dacoit village of Jafarpurwa. Everyone in Jafarpurwa made their living off one form of crime or another. Some ran little gambling dens: dingy mud huts where cards were played for money every day. Others ran illegal liquor dens, brewing the hooch themselves from the cores of rotting fruit. Many, however, just lurked by roadsides after dark, preying on foolhardy travellers like Simha. Armed with bamboo poles and spears, gangs of dark, swarthy men would loot any and every one passing by, stripping them of all that was of any value and then melting away into the night.

A word of protest or, God forbid, a move to fight them and they would not hesitate to use their sharp-edged blades. One flick of the wrist, and a life would be snuffed out, left bleeding by the highway for scavenging animals, or the police to find the following day. A cyclist on the canal road near Kathawa village was once killed simply because he had said *'kahan ja rahe ho bhaiya'* (where are you going brother). For them it was inauspicious if they were addressed from behind. At home, the little children in Jafarpurwa spent their days playing, the older ones learning the tricks of their fathers' trade. If they went to school at all, it was for a few cursory days, till they tired of the routine.

Ironically, it was Birbal's son Ramswaroop who first began to change Jafarpurwa. He didn't preach or rail against the crime and vice. He just walked to our school every day from the time he was a little boy of ten, clutching a ragged little notebook as if his life depended upon it. In school, he would drink in every word, his brow furrowing in concentration as he took copious notes. At the end of the day, he would pick up his book and walk home. He had no friends, and didn't linger after class to roughhouse with the other kids. I have a feeling he just wanted to get back home and finish his homework before dark.

After passing Class 10 (the first boy from Jafarpurwa to pass the Class 10 examination) from our school, Ramswaroop went to Lucknow to study further. Nirmala and I were so proud. He should celebrate, we told him, as we grinned our congratulations. He smiled a little smile at all the fuss, then turned around and left. We didn't see him for two years after that, and then, suddenly one afternoon he walked back into our school. 'I have been admitted to Lucknow University,' he said quietly, with that little smile playing on his lips. 'I'm doing my BA in sculpture and I plan to get a master's in Fine Arts. I want to make statues for a living.'

Birbal had hated the idea of his son going to school. He didn't believe that a dacoit's son could be anything but a dacoit, and he didn't want his young boy wasting his time trying to learn things that would never be of any use to him. He also worried that the entire village would laugh at the young man who had tried to be someone else. As it transpired, the entire village also yearned to be someone else.

Things changed very rapidly in Jafarpurwa after Ramswaroop's education. Parents began bringing their children to our school, asking whether we could teach them. Today, all the children from the village are in school, many of them at our little establishment in Kunaura. Many of the older ones have moved to Lucknow. Some have got that most coveted of occupations, a government job. Two of them taught in our school till last year when they found better jobs. Some, making the most of their tough physique and generations of fitness training, have even joined the police force.

* * *

My sons were now teenagers and I was glad to see them learning to think for themselves, ignoring even my prejudices and stereotypes. One evening, they were playing cricket with a group of children in a field next to our house. When they returned, I asked why had picked Kalu, a sweeper's son, for their team.

'If you want us to play with Mohit [the Brahmin boy next door] instead, we will,' said Shailesh, 'but Kalu is better than him ... at cricket and in school.' I began to think about what I had said, the assumptions I had made, and marvelled at the wisdom of my young boys.

It didn't really surprise me when Neelesh became a journalist in later years. From the time he was a boy, that child just couldn't resist a newspaper, to the extent that he would stop on the way to school with his schoolbag on his back and read a piece of newspaper lying on the road if it dealt with anything of interest. In college, he would contribute poems to his college magazine and even to a children's magazine called *Target* published by the India Today group. When he was about sixteen, he used to say he wanted to start a printing press and publish his own magazine. I explained to him that you could publish a magazine without actually owning a printing press. He very solemnly agreed to amend his plans accordingly.

As a family with adolescent boys, it wasn't easy to find fun things we could all do together, especially in the sleepy Nainital of the 1980s. Then television came to town. Of course, in those days, television wasn't the feast of digitally enhanced choices it is today. Reception was very poor and the only channel available was the government-run Doordarshan, which had erratic standards on entertainment programmes and only the government's view on the news.

All that changed for a few glorious hours every Sunday, when Ramanand Sagar's *Ramayan* would come on. This brilliant film-maker's televized reproduction of the nation's favourite Hindu epic held the country riveted for years. As entire joint families of up to thirty people crowded into their sitting rooms, the gods and goddesses of Hindu lore would appear on their screens, draped in gold and fancy headdresses, charging across battlefields in their chariots, and shooting the most ornate arrows at one another in the epic battle of good against evil.

For many, it was a quasi-religious experience, akin to a visit to a temple. I believe some of the actors playing the deities were beseeched for blessings on the streets of Mumbai where they lived. The women playing the goddesses couldn't get other roles because no one wanted to see them in their human form! The serial actually increased the demand for television sets manifold.

In Nainital, the ritual of watching *Ramayan* was preceded by another not-so-fun one: trying to get better reception. There were only a few spots on the roof where the TV antennae could catch a signal. Therefore, every Sunday morning, in homes across the little hill station, children would be ordered to the roof to turn the antenna as the adults shouted directions to them from below.

Then, in 1984, there came a time when TV caused a riot. On 31 October, our prime minister, Indira Gandhi, was gunned down by her own Sikh bodyguards as she left home to go to work. As images of her bullet-riddled body were played over and over on TV, the sorrow turned to violent rage, sparking riots against Sikhs across the country.

In Delhi, Lucknow, and many other north Indian cities, young men marched down the streets, shouting slogans of revenge.

'*Khoon ka badla khoon se lenge* (We will avenge blood with blood),' they shouted, as they dragged Sikhs out of their homes and set fire to them, their homes, and their shops. As the violence and arson spread, many Sikhs fled, selling their property at throwaway prices to seek refuge with relatives abroad. Who knows how many Sikhs would have been left if the violence had continued much longer. Then, however, Indira's son Rajiv went on national television, appealing to his people, his mother's people, to 'stop the madness'. As thousands watched the grieving young man put his own loss aside to plead for peace in his country, no one seemed to have an excuse for the hatred any longer.

I had a few Sikh friends and had in fact even stayed at Gurudwara Reetha Sahib, a very revered temple for the Sikhs, situated in the Kumaun hills, during one of my visits to the interiors for my geological field-work. I found the people very hospitable. Indeed, the people of the hills were generally simple, hospitable, and caring. Whenever I reached a village in the evening during my geological treks, they would insist I spend the night there and leave only the next morning. Perhaps their good nature stemmed from their serene surroundings. The hills were so beautiful, untouched and teeming with wildlife. I remember when my field attendant and I were drinking water from a clear stream one summer afternoon (we had exhausted all our own drinking water), we looked across a glade of trees to see a shady den obviously inhabited by a wild animal. There were some bones at the entrance, and perhaps even little ones inside, I remember thinking. We moved away quietly so as not to disturb them.

On another occasion, in the winter, I ran into a clump of trees with some deer resting in the shade. A few metres away, the rest of the herd was basking in the sun and nibbling on the grass on a hillock presenting the very picture of serenity. I noticed that a succession of rocks not far from the spot at Gairkhet contained fossils. Although of more or less of the same age as those in Newfoundland, they are different from them. I am endeavouring to interpret the fossils afresh.

* * *

It was at around this time that I began having phantom heart attacks. To this day, no one believes it was anything more than gas, but I know better ... I had palpitations all the time, I was weak, and I felt afraid to put one foot ahead of the other for fear of a full-blown attack. My doctors all thought I was being hysterical. 'Misraji, how many times, in your opinion, can a person have a heart attack,' my friend and house owner Ram Singh Rawat asked me. 'Once, twice ...,' I ventured, now more worried than ever. 'Surely not more than three times? And you say you feel these palpitations several times a day,' he smiled smugly. 'If that were true, your heart should have stopped long ago.' I didn't find this line of reasoning in the least bit amusing.

Well, he seemed to be correct. My ECG did return normal but I was not convinced. After all, these tests and fancy doctors are wrong all the time, and how did you find out? When you keeled over on the street and your children were left orphaned and your wife widowed, God forbid.

Mrs Shah, the teacher at St Mary's College who had harangued me till I got my boys into St Joseph's school, was with me on this one, God bless her. 'I think you are right,' she told me, lips pursed with concern. 'If you are feeling something is wrong, then something is wrong. What do the doctors know? I tell you, it is surely low blood pressure. Bone marrow soup: that is the solution for all such weakness.' Oh no! but I don't eat meat, I pleaded. 'I gave it up in Canada. I haven't touched a dead animal since. I am most reluctant to try soup made from bone marrow.'

Mrs Shah had however already toddled off to make the preparation. She returned with a large, steaming bowl that made me more nauseous than I had felt in weeks. I feel strange about this, I told her. I don't want to drink the soup made of marrow. 'Would you rather die than sip a little harmless soup,' she challenged. 'Take it, for the sake of your family, for your beautiful boys [oh God, not that again].' In the hills,' she concluded, with a sniff, 'it is an offence to return meat.' Her haranguing had worked once again. I took a few sips and assured her I was feeling much better. The truth is that despite her good intentions, the soup hadn't really helped.

My friend Dr M.P. Singh of Lucknow University dropped by our department in Nainital to take some practical exams at this time, and he suggested I get myself examined at Lucknow Medical College. He brought me back to the city with him and got me admitted to the cardiology ward under his friend Dr Puri. He prescribed some medicines and referred me to a doctor in Nainital in the event of my having any further problems. 'Aha,' I thought. 'So it wasn't all a figment of my imagination after all.' The medicines however didn't help.

By now, Nirmala was getting seriously concerned (finally ... I thought). She took me to Vivekanand Polyclinic in Lucknow, where I was once again admitted for a battery of tests. The doctors here said it was stress. They gave me a placebo, told Nirmala, and I felt instantly better. The verdict: my problem was purely psychological. They gave me some medicines and kept me at the hospital for observation, but I had quite a reaction to the pills. Suddenly one night I began shivering; trembling with cold from head to toe. Finally, a doctor on emergency duty arrived and gave me an antidote. The next morning I checked out of the polyclinic.

I now headed to the clinic of Dr J.L. Suri, whom I had known for quite a while. He saw the prescription and laughed: I had been taking some kind of strong sedative intended for lunatics! The aches and weakness were just the result of gas, Dr Suri told me, smiling. He gave me a course of medicines and about two weeks later I was fine. Well, the palpitations stopped too, though the doctors still insist there never were any.

* * *

In the spring of 1987, Simharao invited Nirmala and me to Andhra Pradesh to see the good work some of his friends were doing with tribals there. It was fascinating to see how other people had tried to uplift those around them. The first project we visited was run by V.B. Chandrasekhar, a Brahmin from Tamil Nadu. Chandrasekhar had married a tribal and later a Kamma girl. He had children from both wives.

His project was located on either side of the Sabari river, a tributary of the Godavari. The project focused on adult education and motivating tribal women to save 10 per cent of their earnings, tribals being known to be poor savers, earning just enough to feed their urge for hooch and tobacco. The money the tribal women collected in Chandrasekhar's programme was then pooled, and accessible to any of them as small, interest-free loans. If they had an idea for a small-scale enterprise or cottage industry they wished to be part of, the government would match the grant from the pool and help them set up shop.

The Chandrasekhars and Simha were also working on a water management campaign. Simha had already constructed twenty check dams in the region, and prepared proposals for a number of others with the help of various funding agencies. Next, Chandrasekhar took us to see his one-time associate, a man nicknamed Gandhi Babu, who had set up an organization to promote education, forest management, and bee-keeping as an alternative means of employment in the non-crop seasons.

This project was set up in an isolated place accessible only via the river. Nirmala and I were escorted by Simharao on to a boat that then drifted down the Godavari to the picturesque hamlet of Vararamachandrapuram, where we spent the night. The following morning we started off again, stopping at various villages to pick up other passengers, much as would a bus or a train. The boat carried everything: goats, humans, chickens, grain, and had a kitchen of some kind for those travelling long distances. For a few rupees more, you could get meals on board: delicious rice, sambhar, and stewed vegetables served on banana leaves.

Simha had told me during his recent visit to us that a dam is now being built across the river near Papikondalu, where the two banks of lush green vegetation come so close to each other. They tell me the dam will end the pleasurable boat rides along the river, and the lush green vegetation and forests on one side will vanish forever.

At Rampachodavaram village, we got off the boat and met a social worker called Shiva Ram Krishna. Krishna had a PhD in tribal folklore and was running an NGO called Sakti (Strength). With some help from a UK NGO, Krishna was helping protect springs and other small water sources. Then there was the Bhagawatula Charitable Trust, my favourite. This NGO was started by Bhagawatula Bala Parmeshwar Rao with a grant of Rs 10,000 from his father. Bhagawatula is a nuclear physicist and worked in the US for a while, but had always yearned to return home and help rebuild his country. He therefore decided to try and set things up in the US before returning and fulfilling his dream. He sought an appointment with Robert McNamara, then president of the World Bank, and explained his dream of setting up a school in his village. Years later, when McNamara visited India, he asked Indira Gandhi if she knew of this man and his project. Indiraji had him tracked down with great difficulty, and invited him to meet McNamara in Delhi.

When we visited Bhagawatula, his little school had expanded into a high school, and he was also helping convert barren hill slopes into lush farmland with special agricultural techniques he had seen at work in the US. 'There are no wastelands in India, only wasted lands,' he used to say.

On our return to Secunderabad, a friend of Chandrasekhar invited us to Maharashtra Mandal in Hyderabad. It was a well-organized NGO run by Maharashtrians which ran a school and organized a number of socio–cultural activities. When I told them the story of our school at Kunaura, they were surprised that Nirmala and I had been able to pull off such a difficult project on our own in such an isolated place, with no team to help us with administration or finance, on the basis of just our own resources and time. It was nice to sit with people who had been through the same struggles as the two of us, been consumed by the same motivation, and had triumphed against the odds, abandoning their personal ambition in order that others could have a shot at theirs.

credit denied, again

In 1988, my sons passed out of high school from St Joseph's. It was now time for them to select a college and a career. Unfortunately, Neelesh showed no inclination to become a doctor, a healer of the sick and the poor, a dream I had long envisioned for my brilliant boy. He instead wanted to study the humanities. What good would that do, I pleaded. Where was there a career for people who had spent their college years reading about the past, or studying ancient civilizations? He wouldn't listen. Desperate, I tried to pander to his ego. You have a brilliant mind, I would tell him. You must not waste it. Think of all the good you can do as a famous doctor, like the wealthy, well-respected father of that girl you first made friends with in school. But nothing helped. I blamed the science and maths teachers at the Nainital school. They were not good enough and now my son had lost interest in the serious subjects.

Nirmala and I got the boys admitted to Mahanagar Boys' School in Lucknow with the fond hope that Neelesh would revive his interest in science. This school was supposed to have great science and maths teachers. That didn't help either. I eventually made a deal with Neelesh: If he got a First Class (60 per cent or more), he could study the subject of his choice; if he didn't, the choice would be mine. Neelesh got a First Class and opted for a bachelor of arts degree from Kumaun University in Nainital where I was teaching. Shailesh too decided to return to Nainital, to the government inter-college.

Once I had reconciled myself to Neelesh's choices, it was more or less smooth going. Both boys graduated five years later and Neelesh went to Delhi to prepare for the IAS exam. An IAS officer was almost as good as a doctor, I recall thinking. Well, that wasn't to be either. Just days before his exam, Neelesh was chatting with a family friend and was appalled to discover that, while he imagined he was about to get some sort of plum job with the central government in Delhi, he could in fact be posted pretty much anywhere, doing virtually anything for the entire duration of his career. That didn't sound like the kind of life he wanted so, scouting around for options, he filled out a form for the Indian Institute of Mass Communication at the premier Jawaharlal Nehru University campus.

He is a journalist in his own right now, and also uses his creativity to write the most beautiful lyrics and scripts for Bollywood films. In addition, he has recently set up India's first writer-led band, with Bollywood artistes. He has proved me wrong. Apparently, a lot of good can come from studying the humanities.

Shailesh followed a straight path: getting an MBA from Lucknow University and going on to become a software engineer with Adobe, the well-known American software company. He is now a manager there.

* * *

I seem to always have trouble with people stealing the credit for my work. In Nainital, in the late 1980s, it happened again. Professor K.S. Valdiya, the head of the geology department, reproduced my research material on the Nainital hills without my permission, or credit. I filed a formal complaint to him with a copy to the university registrar.

An enquiry committee was constituted to look into the matter, but in the meantime Professor Valdiya had become officiating vice chancellor and I was never informed about the outcome. It was 1989 and a lot was being written by John Talent, an Australian scientist, and others about V. J. Gupta of Chandigarh University, who allegedly plagiarized research work on Himalayan fossils. Gupta had become internationally infamous and I wondered why Professor Valdiya had not learnt a lesson. Instead, he went on the defensive and sniffed in a workshop on the Ediacaran fossils in Nainital, in a most injured manner, that he had been 'put in the dock'. I had brought up the matter before a gathering of eminent Indian scientists but he knew of ways of extricating himself from an uncomfortable situation of this nature. Years later, he left the department and went to Bangalore and the matter was never discussed again.

I was planning to retire from the university as my wife was in Lucknow looking after the school and my sons had also completed their education at Nainital, there was no particular incentive to stay on. In 1997, I became dean of the Science Faculty, but midway through my term I decided to avail of the option to retire at the age of fifty-eight. Dr O.P. Goel, now head of the department, was keen that I continue but all I wanted now was to return home to my wife and my village school. In 1998, I finally returned to Kunaura.

With part of my retirement benefits, I started a little dairy farm on our land at Kunaura. With free fodder coming from the land and the manure being used as fertilizer, it was a win–win situation. The milk was sold to government collection centres, bringing in extra money.

A year earlier, Nirmala and I had met Sharat Pradhan, a journalist friend of Neelesh's who knew the then secretary of Basic Education. He helped us get an appointment with the secretary and I explained to him how, decades after we started our venture, the school had still not made it to the list of institutions eligible for government grants although we had fulfilled all the conditions. The secretary, Alok Ranjan, gave us a patient hearing and said he would 'take it as a test case'. A few weeks later, we finally made it to that list. From now on, the government would pay the salaries of five teachers, a clerk, and a peon. They even paid us arrears for the previous financial year.

We had lost a number of excellent teachers to government schools because they needed the higher pay. It was good to know this would never happen again, at least in the Junior High School section. Now, the most loyal ones received the same salaries right in their own village, and we ensured distribution of the arrears at the earliest.

Sadly, Nirmala's father, who had dedicated nearly twenty-five years to our school, passed away in July 1998, before he could see the fortunes of our project turn around.

Nirmala had been having some problems with funds for the midday meals for our school kids. For a few years, we had been running this scheme on donations and had been receiving just sufficient for snacks for about 200 children, who would line up every afternoon for some sprouted grain or roasted gram and puffed rice. Occasionally, as most of them were so undernourished, we would treat them to some fruits. Over the past few years, however, the number of students had more than doubled, to over four hundred. We were now able to give the kids only token fistfuls of puffed rice, sometimes with roasted gram and peanuts.

This scheme of midday refreshment was being funded by Satya Gupta, a widow and disciple of Swami Pathikji who had helped us build some of the rooms for Bharatiya Gramin Vidyalaya when permanent recognition was stuck on the grounds of the lack of a building. Satya Gupta was generous enough to feed our kids, though funds provided by her were inadequate for the increasing number of students.

It was around this time that Neelesh met Swami Chidanand Saraswati in Varanasi where he was attending an event organized in honour of the Dalai Lama. Neelesh mentioned our project to swamiji who wanted us to meet him. At Rishikesh, we met Swami Chidanand and got talking about the school and our efforts of decades to provide education to a deprived area. Swamiji promised to help and, a few days later, referred us to Beena Stevenson, a disciple of his.

She offered a huge donation, and promised more on condition that the school be named after the trust named after her father, the Chhotu Ram Tulsi Das Foundation. I agreed to rename our unaided project the CTD Foundation School, and it has been running under that name ever since. Beenaji, for her part, funded four more classrooms, an office, and seven toilets. We still had no secondary classes, but now we had the best primary school for miles. Beena even helped us fund a tailoring course, buying six sewing machines on which young women could learn in batches. To this day, about twenty-five such trainees sign up for the course every year, learning cutting and machining, and going on to earn their own living.

Swamiji took a lot of interest in one of my manuscripts too, and had it published under the title *Bharatiyata Aur Paryavaran* (Indianness and the Environment). It was released by the famous spiritual leader Ramesh Bhai Ojha at Paramarth Ashram in Rishikesh. The book is about how most of our ecological problems could have been avoided had we only followed Indian values and lifestyle, blended, of course, with sustainable development. It was exciting to see something I had written brought out as a book, with my name on the cover. I didn't know it then, but my name was about to adorn something even more exciting than that limited edition. After all my struggles for due credit for my work in Newfoundland, one of the four fossil types I had discovered there was going to be named after me: *Fractofusus Misrai*!

a rock after my name

It all began with a visit from a former student, Arun Kumar, in the winter of 1999. Arun was working at Carleton University at that time. He told me he had proudly mentioned my discovery of Ediacaran fossils in Newfoundland to Guy Narbonne, a professor at Queen's University, Ontario. He was quite surprised, he said, when Narbonne apparently brushed aside my claim, saying 'that was just a report'.

Over dinner, I told Arun how Professor M.M. Anderson had tried to claim my work as his own at Memorial University, and how I had fought to reclaim it. I was surprised at Narbonne's comments, I said, because various international journals and publications had repeatedly attributed the findings to me, and scientists from around the world had written in with their congratulations, some asking for copies of my notes and photographs of the fossil samples, which I still possessed. It struck me, after Arun had left, that perhaps the intellectual property that I had reclaimed was lost again after I left Canada, usurped by unscrupulous individuals like Anderson. I therefore decided to investigate and discover why Professor Narbonne was dismissing my role in my own discovery.

My son Shailesh, who was doing an MBA from Lucknow University, had recently bought a computer, and he had an Internet connection. He therefore suggested we Google Narbonne. We found a microsite run by the professor, linked to the Queen's University website. On it, he had discussed my fossils and their immense significance, but attributed the find to 'students and faculty of Memorial University'. I was sitting on a rock, watching the ocean and eating a sandwich, I thought to myself. Where were the students and faculty!

As I read the report on the site, I had the sinking feeling that my great achievement had slipped away years ago and I had not even been aware of it. Someone (probably Anderson, I remember thinking) had seized the opportunity after I left and tagged their name on my work after I returned to my village in Uttar Pradesh. This disturbed me and I discussed the matter with my sons for the first time. Both boys were upset to see me so dejected.

Shailesh immediately began work on a website, clearly staking my claim to the discovery and supporting that claim with my thesis, research papers, and photographs from all those years ago. Neelesh, who was working with the Associated Press, helped us organize a press conference to announce the website and discuss my discovery. A BBC correspondent interviewed me over the phone soon after the press conference, and I told him of my struggle to keep my work from being hijacked, and how the credit for the discovery of an entirely new fauna (organism) was now in danger of being stolen. The reporter called Professor Narbonne too, asking for his reaction to my statements. Narbonne declined to comment.

Our website was, meanwhile, receiving hits from geoscientists around the world, including one from Narbonne, who graciously admitted in an email that he was impressed with the quantity of material presented on it. At about that time, Sharat Pradhan, a senior journalist of Lucknow, had succinctly put the point in an article on Rediff.com on

22 September 2000, in which he said, 'What continues to irk him (me) is that his deductions and observations constituting path-breaking work on the subject were being recycled without acknowledging his role, and that too when there is talk about intellectual property rights.'

I sent an email to Narbonne on 19 May 2000, saying I strongly objected to his statement in his website about the discovery of Mistaken Point Fossils being made by 'students and faculty'. If he had any further questions, I added, I would be glad to answer them as I still had the letters of eminent geoscientists of the time, the original fossils and their casts. There was no reason to give credit to unknown heroes, I wrote in my email.

Narbonne emailed my son soon after, saying he had referred to the website in a publication that was due out soon, and had credited me with the discovery of the fossils at Mistaken Point, calling it 'one of the most important Proterozoic fossil assemblages known'. Narbonne attributed dishonesty not to himself but to others when he said 'I have heard that other people in Newfoundland have not been quite as honest, and have tried to take credit for discoveries they did not make. That is not me.' He asked us to include a link to his website on ours! My son Shailesh, the webmaster, has given the link. Narbonne had eventually corrected his website and replaced the references to students and faculty of Memorial University by 'Remains of soft-bodied animals were discovered at Mistaken Point during the summer of 1967 during the M.Sc. thesis research of S.B. Misra of Memorial University of Newfoundland. Misra's extensive website documents this discovery and contains copies of all of his publications on the subject.'

Professor Narbonne did change his attitude towards me in great measure when he wrote: 'Your role as the discoverer and first interpreter of these fossils has been very firmly established by all subsequent workers, and we have justifiably lauded you for your discoveries.' He went on to say in the same email: 'All of your ideas were valid when they were suggested in 1967'. Soon after, he did a lot more.

***

On 4 August 2007, I received an email from Professor Narbonne, saying he and fellow scientist Dr Jim Gehling of Australia had named one of the four categories of fossils after me: *Fractofusus misrai.* This unique honour about forty years after my discovery took my breath away. The formal announcement was made at a distinguished gathering of parliamentarians and eminent international scientists in Canada, during the inauguration of an international centre for the study of the Ediacaran fossils. The news received extensive coverage in the national and international press. Professor Narbonne himself wrote to me saying he was thrilled to see the extent of international coverage. On 25 November 2007, I was felicitated at my alma mater, the University of Lucknow, by the alumni association, for my work in India and abroad. It was strange to return to those halls fifty years later, talking about my life and achievements as if I were some celebrity. Another moment of joy for Nirmala and me was the felicitation by the governor of Uttar Pradesh, where he also applauded the work we had been doing in the villages of the state.

The international centre was set up at Portugal Cove South, where I had stayed with the family of Hanna Coombs during my research work. The Mistaken Point area where I found my fossils has been declared an ecological reserve by the Government of Newfoundland and Labrador. On the rugged paths where I had wandered as a student, guided tours are now conducted, retracing my steps. Visitors must be accompanied by an official tour guide to protect the remaining fossils, and an order has been passed to expand the reserve to cover a larger area. Home to some of the oldest fossils ever recovered, the Mistaken Point Ecological Reserve is shortlisted for designation as a UNESCO World Heritage Site. Here in Kunaura school many good things were happening and many good people were joining to carry my dream project forward. One day, a young man landed at the village with the same glint in his eyes that I once had.

the arrival of a new visitor

In the failing light of dusk, twenty-seven-year-old Karan Dalal from Mumbai waits for the lights to come back on. He's facing a computer in a small, sparsely furnished room, but it's not his computer or his room. Oh no, the lights never go out in Mumbai, that glittering commercial capital of our superpower-in-the-making. Karan is in our little school in Kunaura, a brave youngster who has given up a dream job in the city to help teach our students, and our teachers, how to use computers. Kunaura, however, only receives power for a maximum of a few hours a day.

Sixty years after we won our Independence, thousands of villages still have no electricity. Villages were once the strength of our country, in days when ministers died in debt and MLAs left behind just a few pieces of wooden furniture in their village homes. MPs don't however die in debt any longer in India, and MLAs generally leave behind a great deal more than a few wooden chairs.

In the evenings, those sufficiently fortunate can catch a glimpse of the Other India on TV: an India in which schools are large buildings with clusters of well-dressed teachers, where cars are bought on the spot for spoilt youngsters who already have an excess of toys and amenities and sea-facing flats can cost the equivalent of an entire village's income for about ten years.

For Karan, this gaping chasm is an opportunity; it is the reason why he turned down several lucrative job offers in the US to come to India. When he first contacted me, I thought he was a sweet boy, well-intentioned, and I waited for him to come to his senses. After all, twenty-seven-year olds don't just throw away a dream job in a bustling city to move to a village where not a single child has ever seen a newspaper, or a TV set. I thanked him for his offer to help teach computers at our school and expected to hear back from him in a few months, perhaps in the form of a polite call at Diwali, contritely wishing me a happy new year. In reality, when Diwali came around, Karan had moved to Lucknow and had been teaching at our school for over two weeks.

He has refused a salary and almost refused leave to go back home for a few days to celebrate the biggest Hindu festival of the year. Although he can only teach in bursts of 15 and 20 minutes, until the power flickers off again, he has never once complained. Instead, in a gesture that is very reminiscent of a young woman I married many years ago, he has determined to solve the problem. Karan's father has just retired as a top official with a major global consulting firm; his mother a textile designer. Like any parents, they were concerned when they first heard of his plan to go to a village no one had heard of to teach in a tiny school in the middle of nowhere. Their son had graduated in computer science and mathematics from the University of Illinois, Urbana, Chamapaign, and lived in that mecca of wealth for four years. They were however also aware that their son had never wanted to be 'just another code monkey', the American slang, I am told, for software programmers. He had always intended to return and teach.

Back in Mumbai, he completed a Law degree (LLB) from Mumbai University, and while working as a director in a large software company, he read a blog post about our school. The blogger was writer Rahul

Pandita, co-author of one of the books my son Neelesh has written. Karan, a regular follower of the blog, posted a comment and Rahul put him in touch with Neelesh. Six months later, the young man had swapped his full-time job for a consultant's post.

He works out of Lucknow from his laptop and uses the proceeds to support himself and buy the odd peripheral for our rickety computer lab. Karan's arrival was a great coincidence; he, a computer engineer, was arriving just when a major software company had donated us fifteen computers to set up a computer lab. Sadly they were all primitive, most did not work and it left a bitter taste in the mouth for us – is this how major corporation did CSR (Corporate Social Responsibility) programmes?

But that challenge handed us bigger dreams.

With the forty-year history of our campaign behind us, my two sons and Karan are now planning the next forty years. They want to start India's first professionally-managed rural newspaper, a programme to create rural computer teachers as we educate rural call centre/ information centre.

They have ambitious plans, and I am thrilled to see that even within the confines of their busy corporate lives, they nurture the same passion that my wife and I have always tried to keep alive.

Our journey was a largely lonesome one, but suddenly we find that a lot of like-minded people are joining the movement, pitching in whatever they can.

Neelesh's friend Adam Gilmore, a scientist with the space agency NASA, recently arrived in the village and spent a day there, holding presentations for the spellbound children. The three young men are trying to set up a social foundation to help similar social projects across South Asia.

Sukanya Rath, a young veteran in the social sector came to know about our work through Facebook and is helping with the library project and possibly bring (proper) computers. Bollywood singer Shilpa Rao, the lead vocalist of Neelesh's band and his friend, spent days visiting the school recently, and the young talented girl who performs around the world sang with great humility before an amazed audience. Yamini Tripathi, a gritty young woman who manages their band and has managed India's top models, was last seen slogging away, painting the doors of a room in the school! In faraway Chicago, senior journalist and author Mayank Chhaya is trying to garner support for the school.

The passion and selfless devotion of these young men and women is very heartwarming.

* * *

Staying miles away from home, I think Karan probably misses his friends in Mumbai and the US, but that is something he refuses to admit. 'You came back from Newfoundland,' he says to me. 'Did you miss it?' He doesn't speak Hindi very well. He spoke to an assembly of 700 (staff and students) on his first visit in July 2009, and says of the experience, 'That was scarier than any interview ever'.

I imagine that little things are difficult to get accustomed to, like the time he cut his finger and had to go all the way to Lucknow for a tetanus shot, or those hot and humid days when the lizards and centipedes begin crawling out of the walls and on to the ground, the windows, the furniture, and anything that offers a little respite from the mugginess of their homes.

The children have grown very fond of Karan, though, as have the staff. In the midday break, he usually disappears in a crowd of eager questions as the children explore the new world he has opened up to them. While some struggle to use the mouse, others marvel at how neat 'their writing' is on the screen.

For the Class 9 and 10 students there is a definite sense of purpose as they struggle to get the hang of Word: save, open, write … save, open, write. As Karan tries to explain email, they struggle to understand how an 'invisible postman' can bring their mail into the little box-shaped machine. Once the Internet arrives, he will show them how it works, and then they won't have to make up games with pebbles during the break: the world will be at their fingertips.

With the addition of a computer lab in the school, a power connection in each classroom, a fair sized library, sports, and other facilities, the students are ready to think ahead. Even school drop-outs are being contacted by us to join one or another of the vocational training programmes that are to be set up by the school and aim for gainful employment.

Karan and I attempted to learn about the ambitions of the students of the school through a survey conducted in November 2009. I am surprised that they have come miles from the 'high school' to which I had aspired!! A large number of them aspire to become doctors, engineers, police officers, and armymen. However, the most popular profession amongst them is teaching (boys 42 per cent and girls 85 per cent). A few of them want to become sportsmen, but only a negligible number wish to be farmers, their parents' profession. This may not be a positive sign because in the event of their failing to get a 'white collar job' they would be frustrated. We have indeed come across many young men and women who passed the high school examination from this school and Intermediate from other distant colleges but failed to pursue further studies. They are in consequence reluctant farmers.

Dr Murthy, now retired as professor of geophysics from Osmania University in Hyderabad, visited the school along with V.V.N. Simharao, one of the group of ten in Ottawa, Canada. Professor Murthy observed, after seeing our survey: 'All those who would like to become *sainiks* or sportsmen happen to be boys, but, there is hardly any difference in the aspirations of boys and girls castewise.'

They were asked to make suggestions if they had any and several of the senior students made interesting ones. They want this school upgraded to the intermediate or graduation level, a boundary wall constructed around the school, more plantation and computer education. The boundary wall has since been completed.

One of the girls in class 8 had said it is her '*tamanna*' (heart's desire) to become a computer engineer. With such hopes and ambitions in the hearts of students and the dedication of young associates like Karan Dalal, I am certain it will be possible to achieve the goal of quality education for the rural poor. This is beginning of the second challenge.

epilogue

As I look back, I see all the crossroads that brought me here, and the many memorable moments along the way. Most of them occurred during the last forty years, since I set up my school in Kunaura.

As I look back, so many faces light up as milestones on this forty-year journey.

I vividly recall the story of Bitto, the daughter of Hardeo Bajpai who used to call me Gandhi Baba when I was a boy. Bitto (Kusma) married a certain Shiv Kumar who was cruel to her and left her. She met us and narrated the story of her torture and agony. We advised her to join our Mahila Condensed Course. She did and passed the high school examination. Nirmala encouraged her to take up a job, which Kusma did. Nirmala had told Kusma 'not to worry, your husband will come and clean your chappals'. Shiv Kumar did come to Shahpur where Kusma is a teacher, built a house, and both are now living there happily.

Another memorable moment was when a Muslim girl came up to us, peered out from under her headscarf, and said: 'This is all I have. Is it enough to learn to write my name?' Gathered in the apron of her dress were coins she had been collecting for eight months: a grand total of Rs 12. It was pouring outside. Najaf Fatima had waded through 3 kilometres of (for her) knee-high water. 'I heard you teach people how to write,' she said, trying to sound impatient to hide her anxiety. 'I've passed Class 5 in my village school, but I can't write.'

Nirmala helped the girl tie the coins into her handkerchief. Then we put her name in our attendance register. Najaf Fatima never paid a fee, and she never missed a class. She finished Class 8 three years later, with one of the highest averages in her batch. She could write a lot more than her own name.

Then there was the day Neelesh and I were sitting in the courtyard behind the school and one of the boys came up to me and said he wanted permission to go home for the day. 'Why,' I asked. The twelve-year old said he had a stomach-ache. A lot of our children had stomach-aches. Often, it was caused by hunger.

'What did you eat in the morning?' I asked him. '*Kuchh nahin* (nothing),' he said. We had no money at this point for midday meals so there was nothing to feed him. As the boy left, Neelesh looked up. 'I want to help,' he said. I suggested he fund scholarships for our brightest girls and boys. Neelesh and NDTV's Nidhi Razdan, a television news anchor, pledged twenty scholarships a year.

One of the first went to Najaf Fatima. She didn't initially understand. Did we want her to pay ... or were we giving her money, she asked, sounding impatient again. 'It's from us; for you. Because you're one of our best students,' I said, 'it's a prize.' A smile spread across her face. 'Why didn't you say so,' she said.

Then there were exclusively scheduled caste villages – Gadela, Jankinagar, Jafarpurwa, Durjanpurwa, and Naigadhia where not a single person could sign their own name when our school opened. The first two students from Jankinagar, Shatrohan and Nattha Ram, completed high school at Kunaura and continued their education, eventually becoming bank managers. I recently met Shatrohan's father Charan. 'He's a bank manager in Varanasi now,' he said, clasping both my hands in his own. We both knew who he was talking about. He rarely spoke of anything but his son. 'Which bank,' I asked. 'It has an English name,' he smiled. 'I don't know how to say it.' Had the Kunaura school not been there,' I asked Charan, 'where would Shatrohan have gone?' He looked at me blankly and asked in return, 'Where would he have gone?'

Then there was Muneesh of Jafarpurwa, the village of ex-dacoits where every child now goes to school. Muneesh completed his MA and turned up at our school again. 'I want to teach,' he said. A number of former students are now teachers at Kunaura. Ram Chandra Bajpai of Shahpur has a post-graduate degree, Surendra Singh of Himmatpurwa and Raj Kumar of Kunaura graduated while teaching at our school. Kavita and Bindu of Ayodhyanagari, both graduates, taught at our school for two years and are now bringing up children of their own.

Many former students are teachers in government and government-aided schools, like Sarla Awasthi and Rampati Pande. Rampati is headmistress at a government primary school in Raipur village in Sitapur *taluk*. She has built a concrete house in Deora and brought up her two sons herself after her husband abandoned her.

Her younger sister Kokila is a teacher in a government school in Ahewa, in Sitapur district. One of our oldest students, Sarla Awasthi of Sulemabad in Barabanki district is a teacher at a government-aided junior high school. Her younger sister Seema works at a government school in Lucknow. Their two brothers also studied at Kunaura. Rajendra Prakash is a compounder at a veterinary hospital; Surendra Prakash manages an orphanage in Lucknow. Contributions in the field of socio–economic activity have been hugely satisfying to us. Groups of women from Ayodhyanagari, Shahpur, Deora, etc., who were given training in food-processing, making *vadi*, papad, *mungaudi* and packing ground condiments, lentils, and other such things, sometimes meet us and describe how they are making the items at home and selling them. Those who received training, both women and girls, are supplementing their family income. Women and farmers who attended agricultural extension programmes express satisfaction, and that itself is deeply rewarding for us.

However, many of the houses are still in darkness, many bellies are empty, and children ill-clothed. The long, long walk continues, and the path ahead remains long and arduous.

index

a very special thanks to

Zara Murao
Without whose help and perseverance this book could not have been completed